Reggie Bush

FOOTBALL SUPERSTARS

Tiki Barber   Joe Montana
Tom Brady   Walter Payton
Reggie Bush   Adrian Peterson
John Elway   Jerry Rice
Brett Favre   Ben Roethlisberger
Eli Manning   Tony Romo
Peyton Manning   Barry Sanders
Dan Marino   LaDainian Tomlinson
Donovan McNabb   Brian Urlacher

FOOTBALL SUPERSTARS

Reggie Bush

Adam Woog

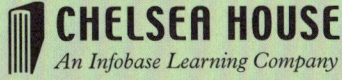

*Special thanks to Tom DeGraff for again
sharing his expertise and enthusiasm. —A.W.*

REGGIE BUSH

Copyright © 2011 by Infobase Learning

All rights reserved. No part of this book may be reproduced or utilized in any form or by any means, electronic or mechanical, including photocopying, recording, or by any information storage or retrieval systems, without permission in writing from the publisher. For information, contact:

Chelsea House
An imprint of Infobase Learning
132 West 31st Street
New York, NY 10001

Library of Congress Cataloging-in-Publication Data
Woog, Adam, 1953–
  Reggie Bush / by Adam Woog.
    p. cm. — (Football superstars)
  Includes bibliographical references and index.
  ISBN 978-1-60413-756-9 (hardcover)
  1. Bush, Reggie, 1985– —Juvenile literature. 2. Football players—United States—Biography—Juvenile literature. I. Title.
  GV939.B836G74 2010
  796.332092—dc22
  [B]
                            2011004492

Chelsea House books are available at special discounts when purchased in bulk quantities for businesses, associations, institutions, or sales promotions. Please call our Special Sales Department in New York at (212) 967-8800 or (800) 322-8755.

You can find Chelsea House on the World Wide Web at http://www.infobaselearning.com

Text design by Erik Lindstrom
Cover design by Ben Peterson and Keith Trego
Composition by EJB Publishing Services
Cover printed by Bang Printing, Brainerd, Minn.
Book printed and bound by Bang Printing, Brainerd, Minn.
Date printed: September 2011
Printed in the United States of America

10 9 8 7 6 5 4 3 2 1

This book is printed on acid-free paper.

All links and Web addresses were checked and verified to be correct at the time of publication. Because of the dynamic nature of the Web, some addresses and links may have changed since publication and may no longer be valid.

CONTENTS

1	Introducing Reggie Bush	7
2	The Early Years	14
3	Growing as an Athlete	24
4	From College to the Pros	38
5	Going to New Orleans	53
6	The 2007 and 2008 Seasons	71
7	The Big Game and the Next Steps	87

Statistics	106
Chronology	107
Timeline	108
Glossary	111
Bibliography	114
Further Reading	118
Picture Credits	119
Index	120
About the Author	126

Introducing Reggie Bush

In his relatively short career, Reggie Bush has emerged as one of the most talented players on the football field. Many observers believe that he has the potential to be among the top running backs of all time.

Bush first gained attention among fans from 2003 to 2005 as a member of the University of Southern California Trojans. During his college years, Bush's team captured two national championships, and he won numerous awards and honors, including the 2005 Heisman Trophy.

Bush left USC a year early to declare for the National Football Leauge (NFL) Draft, and the New Orleans Saints chose him that year with the second pick overall. So far, he has spent his entire pro career with the Saints. (The team is named for a famous song, "When the Saints Go Marching In," that is one of the greatest symbols of the Louisiana city. It is an apt reflection of New Orleans's music-rich history.)

In college and in the NFL, Bush says, he has succeeded because he has simply done what comes naturally—and what he loves. In an article by Kevin Acee in the *San Diego Union-Tribune*, Bush talked about what happens when he is on the field:

> I'm not thinking. I'm just going off instinct. The only thing going through my mind is, "Make this guy miss." I just take it as the play goes on. That's what I do. I'm going to go out and make big plays. I like to do it all. I feel like I'm dangerous when I get the ball in my hands. Returning the ball, catching the ball, running, I like it all. I love to play football.

"... AND THEN THERE'S REGGIE BUSH"

Many fans and commentators have put Bush in the same bracket of talent as the best backs in NFL history. Among these legends are Gale Sayers, Barry Sanders, Tony Dorsett, and Marshall Faulk.

The comparisons to Sayers, nicknamed "The Kansas Comet," may be the closest. Like Sayers, Bush shines when he is out in space—that is, in the open field. Also like Sayers, Bush is blindingly fast, with an innate ability to cut back and leave would-be tacklers in his wake.

In addition, Bush has proven time and again that he can be a remarkably versatile player. Over the years, he has been outstanding not only as a running back but also as a wide receiver and a punt returner. (Furthermore, he was a track star in high school.) Nonetheless, Bush remains most impressive as a running back/tailback.

Bush—sometimes called "the President" because he shares a last name with two former U.S. presidents—is relatively small for the position he plays. He stands 6 feet tall (1.83 meters) and weighs some 203 pounds (92 kilograms). In terms of sheer

NFL running back Reggie Bush is known for his speed and agility on the field. After joining the New Orleans Saints in 2006, Bush established himself as one of the NFL's most talented players.

bulk, he would never compare with some of football's heftiest and most bruising backs.

Nonetheless, Bush is just as fearsome a presence on the field as they are. As fellow USC and NFL back Anthony Davis put it, in an article by *Sports Illustrated* journalist Phil Taylor, "There are dangerous backs, there are very dangerous backs, and then there's Reggie Bush."

"SAINT REGGIE"

But to many fans—especially those in the New Orleans area—Bush has been much more than just a talented football player. When he arrived for his rookie year with the Saints, he was

"BLINDING" AND "RIDICULOUS"

Since high school, straight through his college career, and into the pros, Reggie Bush has inspired high praise from sportswriters and other commentators with his amazing athleticism. Here are a few typical examples:

Arash Markazi, *Daily Trojan*: "Reggie Bush looks like a creation from a video game—an almost unreal character created by a kid who finds all the secret codes to make his player faster, quicker, and better than everyone else on the field. . . . He always makes the impossible seem possible. The scary thing for . . . opponents is that this creation isn't imaginary. He's not from a video game. He's a living, breathing human joystick who terrorizes defenses with his blinding speed and ankle-breaking shimmies. . . . Bush's speed borders on blinding and his knack for eluding defenders borders on ridiculous."

David Leon Moore, *USA Today*: "Reggie Bush is basically a sworn enemy of a straight line. He's all switchbacks and seen as someone who could help the city recover from a terrible natural disaster.

Bush came to New Orleans not long after Hurricane Katrina devastated the region, leaving hundreds dead and thousands homeless. The region was experiencing widespread anger over government inaction during and after the storm, and residents had precious little hope. One of the few bright spots for the city was the expectation that its football team could pull out of its slump—and that "Saint Reggie," as he was nicknamed, was the man for the job.

Bush's performance during his rookie year was spectacular—everything that had been hoped for. He played a key

> zigzags, spin moves and ankle-breaking shimmies. . . . He is a quiet sort, polite, humble, good grades, solid citizen [but] on a football field, he gets around like nobody else. Here, there, this sideline, that end zone, he's running, receiving, returning, making plays, scoring touchdowns, winning games. . . . He runs with a can't-take-your-eyes-off-him style that seems part Marshall Faulk, part Barry Sanders, part Gale Sayers."
>
> Todd Harmonson, *Orange County Register*: "Reggie Bush is a highlight-show fixture with physiology-defying, did-he-do-that moves. The easy comparison is to Marshall Faulk because of the similarity in all-around games, but those who saw Gale Sayers recognize the speed, spins and spellbinding cuts. . . . Reggie Bush is a speed demon who sees Christmas morning when a linebacker tries to defend him and a winnable challenge when a quick corner draws the assignment."

When Bush joined the New Orleans Saints in 2006, the city was still recovering from Hurricane Katrina, a devastating natural disaster. Bush and his teammates pulled the Saints out of a years-long slump, which helped provide entertainment and tourism to New Orleans.

role in leading a once luckless team close to an appearance in the Super Bowl and then, a few years later, help the Saints become Super Bowl champions for the first time in their history. Furthermore, he has become a hero to many in New Orleans by giving generously from his newfound wealth to help rebuild the city.

Bush, however, has also come under considerable criticism—notably for his erratic record on the field. He was also the target of close scrutiny over allegations that he accepted improper gifts and money when he was a college student.

Nonetheless, Bush has remained to many a bright star of the game, in New Orleans and beyond. Journalist Arash

Markazi, writing in *Sports Illustrated*, summed up the opinion of many fans when he noted:

> What separates Bush from many of his peers is that he doesn't pad his stats against bad teams in blowout wins. He rises to the occasion when his team needs him most. When they are against ranked teams, when they are on the road, when they are behind, when they are in need of a lift, Bush is always there to place his teammates firmly on his back and carry them to yet another win.

FAMILY TIES

Bush has always been close to his family, and he is quick to credit them for their unswerving support and help. In particular, he says, their strong religious faith and personal values have helped him thrive—both in the grueling world of pro football and in the glitzy world of celebrity that he has joined.

After a game, he tries to avoid reporters, often preferring to meet with or call his parents. They say that their son invariably asks their opinion about his performance. The Bush family attends as many games as possible, proudly wearing personalized versions of his jersey. Their support, coupled with the athlete's innate gifts, has helped take him to remarkable heights. The journey to these heights began in San Diego, California, in 1985.

The Early Years

Reggie Bush's road to football began on March 2, 1985. That's the day Reginald Alfred Bush II was born at Sharp Memorial Hospital in San Diego, California. Reggie's birthplace, San Diego, is south of Los Angeles on the Pacific Ocean, close to the U.S. border with Mexico.

The baby was named after his biological father. Reggie Bush Sr. was a native of the small town of Indianola, Mississippi. He grew up, however, in two big cities: Chicago, Illinois, and Los Angeles.

While attending Hawthorne High School in Los Angeles, Reggie Sr. proved to be a talented athlete. Like his son would be, he was a running back on the football team.

Also similar to his son, Reggie Sr. was known for having unusual speed. In fact, he was nicknamed "Dancing Man" for his quick feet. For a variety of reasons, however, Reggie Sr.'s playing career did not go past high school.

YOUNG PARENTS

Reggie Sr. was living in Los Angeles when he met Reggie's mother, Denise Lewis, who was also athletic and had played basketball in high school.

Although she grew up in a strongly religious household, Denise admits now that she went through a wild period when she was a teenager. This included getting pregnant with Reggie Sr.'s child, which happened when they were both young. He was only 20, and she was only 19.

Unfortunately, Denise's pregnancy created a lot of tension between the two. In an interview with journalist Doug Krikorian during his son's college career, reprinted on the Web site thefreelibrary.com, Reggie Bush Sr. acknowledged, "We were young at the time, and I wasn't really ready to be a father."

As a result, they split up when Denise was only a few months pregnant. She moved south to her mother's home in the Skyline area of San Diego and stayed there after her baby was born.

When Reggie was seven months old, he and Denise moved out of her mother's house. She rented an apartment for the two of them in Imperial Beach, a small town just north of the Mexican border.

Soon after this move, Denise met a young man named LaMar Griffin at a dance club. They began to date and fell in love. LaMar and Denise got married when Reggie was still a toddler. The family settled in Spring Valley, a suburb just east of San Diego. LaMar adopted Reggie, and Reggie has called him "Dad" all of his life.

Together, Denise and LaMar had another son, Reggie's younger half brother Jovan. Like Reggie, Jovan was an athletic boy. He grew up to be several inches taller (but more slender) than his older brother and has become a notable athlete. Reggie also has two half sisters, Doniele and Dezhane, Reggie Sr.'s daughters by a later marriage.

A DIFFICULT RELATIONSHIP

When Reggie was young, he found it difficult to have a biological father who was largely absent. For one thing, Reggie Sr. did not visit him often. Also, Reggie Sr. apparently did not live up to his financial agreement with Denise. Official records show that Denise had to go to court to get him to pay child support for his son.

Reggie Sr. has had only limited contact with his son. In an article in the *Los Angeles Times* by David Wharton, his son said, "It was tough with both sides of the family not getting along too well. [I was] caught in a tug-of-war."

Nonetheless, Reggie Sr. asserts now that he played a significant role in his son's life when the future star was young. Still, there is little evidence to back up that statement. The two continue to have a difficult relationship.

Reggie Sr. says that he is proud of his famous son and is grateful that the boy was raised well by Denise and LaMar. On a Web site he maintained for a while, the older Bush acknowledged this positive upbringing. He wrote, "He has a tremendous mother and stepfather, and they provided for him very well. Very well. I thank God for Denise and LaMar Griffin. They deserve the best."

"CHORES EVERY WEEKEND"

LaMar and Denise have been caring, strong, and protective parents. They made sure that Reggie and his brother grew up well. Denise and LaMar expected a lot from their boys—among other things, they insisted that their sons study hard in school, remain modest and truthful, and stay out of trouble.

Both LaMar and Denise were hard workers, and they passed their work ethic on to the boys. Denise had a job at

The Early Years 17

While he was growing up, Bush was not in regular contact with his biological father but was raised in a loving home created by his mother Denise and his stepfather LaMar Griffin.

the local chapter of the Humane Society and was later a correctional officer at the Vista Detention Facility, a county jail. Meanwhile, LaMar worked as a security officer at Samuel F.B. Morse High School (which had been Denise's school).

These jobs did not earn the family a great deal of money, and finances were always a little tight. The Griffins were far from poor, but nonetheless they had few luxuries. In an interview in *Men's Fitness* magazine, Reggie recalled that this situation was one reason he wanted to become a successful athlete. He commented, "We couldn't really go shopping. I only had one new pair of shoes. Part of my motivation to succeed was just that I wanted to be able to shop when I wanted. Part of it was to never have to live like I lived growing up."

Besides being hard workers, both of Reggie's parents were deeply religious. In fact, LaMar was a minister. They played an important role in introducing their sons to a spiritual way of living and thinking. In this manner, they laid the groundwork for the strong sense of purpose and morality that Reggie has maintained as an adult.

Furthermore, they taught their sons the importance of respect and thoughtfulness. Both Denise and LaMar had been raised in strict households where family members instilled these qualities in them. In an article by journalist David Wharton in the *Los Angeles Times*, Denise Griffin recalled, "My parents were so strict. You had to say 'Yes, sir' and 'Yes, ma'am.' You did not talk back."

The Griffins raised Reggie and Jovan in the same firm but loving way. If the boys forgot to make their beds before leaving the house, for instance, their father would chase after them and make them come back. In the Wharton article, Reggie recalled that his mother and father were "[n]ot too strict, but they stayed on top of us. I had to do my homework and clean my room. Chores every weekend."

STARTING POP WARNER FOOTBALL

As a boy, Reggie was unusually athletic and seemed to be active all the time. In fact, he was so active that one of his teachers suggested to his parents that maybe he needed medication to calm down. Reggie, however, never needed such medicine. Instead, he started to put all of that energy to good use. He started to play football.

Reggie's entry into the world of football can be traced to his love for the energetic games that he played with other kids in the neighborhood. His mother remembers that, during games like keep-away, he began to do the spectacular spinning and cutting moves he would later display on the football field. In a 2005 article in *Sports Illustrated*, his mother recalled, "He'd get such a kick out of faking them out—he would just crack up. He still gets joy from that."

When Reggie was nine, his stepfather enrolled him in a Pop Warner league. LaMar hoped that it would help Reggie direct his energy into a fun and positive activity. The team was called the Grossmont/La Mesa Mighty Mite Warriors.

At first Denise Griffin was concerned about her son playing a rough game like football. She worried because he sometimes had difficulty breathing. Initially, she and LaMar simply thought that Reggie just got out of breath from running

"A GIFT FROM GOD"

The deep religious faith of Reggie Bush's family and church elders was important in shaping his unassuming outlook on life and sports. Katie Woods is the senior pastor at the family's church, and she has continued to be a spiritual mentor to Bush. In an article in the *San Diego Union-Tribune* by Brent Schrotenboer, she said: "I tell his family to remind him that no matter what he does, no matter how much media attention, no matter how famous he gets to be, that if he just stays humble and remembers that if all of this was given to him as a gift from God, that he can't lose."

Bush's mother will often send him (by e-mail, voice message, or text) a religious quotation to consider. Meanwhile, his stepfather, LaMar Griffin, is himself a minister and has often directed him toward important biblical verses. For example, when Bush was in high school, his stepfather gave him a specific verse to consider, Matthew 23:12: "Whoever exalts himself will be humbled, and whoever humbles himself will be exalted."

around. In a newspaper article by Brent Schrotenboer, LaMar Griffin said, "We didn't recognize it at first because Reggie used to just rip and run."

As it turned out, Reggie was suffering from asthma. The asthma went away in time, but Denise had other health concerns. For instance, Reggie was slender, and she worried that he would not be able to hold his own while playing against bigger, stronger boys. In Wharton's *Los Angeles Times* article, Denise recalled, "He was a tall, slim kid. I was like, 'Oh, he's going to get hurt.'"

"HE WAS JUST SO MUCH BETTER"

With some difficulty, LaMar and Reggie managed to convince Denise that he would be fine. As it turned out, she did not need to worry. In fact, Reggie learned quickly and demonstrated right away that he had phenomenal speed and instincts.

In his first game, in September 1994, he rushed six times, five of them for touchdowns, for 203 yards. The next month he played in his first official game, a 53-37 victory over the Kearny Mesa Komets. During the game, Reggie rushed for 544 yards on 27 carries, kicked three extra points, scored eight touchdowns, caught one pass, made two tackles, and recovered a fumble—all in a 32-minute game.

Reggie earned a photo in the local paper for this feat. In Schrotenboer's article in the *San Diego Union-Tribune*, the team's statistician, Allen Barbour, recalled, "It was mind-boggling." LaMar Griffin added in an interview in the *New York Times*, "I couldn't believe what I saw."

Reggie continued to put on an impressive show throughout his Pop Warner years. Video from those days shows Reggie outrunning everybody else. He had a knack for twisting and cutting to find open space. Nicknamed "The Cutback King," he averaged 19.3 yards per carry.

In a *San Diego Union-Tribune* article, Reggie's coach, Paul Lane, recalled that his moves in Pop Warner ball were remarkably similar to those he would make as an adult pro footballer. Lane said, "He looked the same when he was nine years old as he does today. We tried to coach him down a little so he wouldn't get a big head. He was just so much better than anybody else."

A GAME HE WAS MEANT TO PLAY

Today, Reggie credits his parents' support for keeping him going during these early years. He says now that he would have failed if they had not been behind him, urging him to stick with football and stay out of trouble. In an article in *Men's Fitness* magazine, he remarked:

> There were 10 guys just as good as me. They didn't make it. They got caught up in gangs. They had nobody to push them.... Everyone doesn't have an equal opportunity growing up, but don't let it be an excuse. Use it as motivation.

Reggie has also commented that he had a hard time understanding why everyone was so surprised he did well. To him, he was only doing what came naturally. In an article in the *Los Angeles Times*, he said, "I was playing a game I loved. A game I was supposed to play."

In fact, as Reggie got older, he had a persistent feeling that he was somehow fated to excel at football. One evening when he was a junior in high school, his mother was in their living room watching a Christian evangelist on television. Reggie was doing his homework at the kitchen table and could hear the program.

The preacher was talking about how some people feel anointed to do certain things. His mother did not realize that

Reggie was listening to the TV until he walked into the living room. In an interview with journalist Kevin Acee, Reggie recalled that he looked up and told his mother, "That's how I feel about football."

STUDYING OTHERS

Reggie was able to enhance his obvious natural talent by watching outstanding players and studying how they moved. For example, he closely followed the career of Marshall Faulk, a star running back at San Diego State University during this period. (Faulk went on to become an All-Pro player for the Indianapolis Colts and the St. Louis Rams.) Reggie tried to copy Faulk's running style. Furthermore, by watching Faulk, Reggie could see that a running back who was smaller than average could still dominate a game.

Reggie admired the many gridiron stars who came from the San Diego area. Among these athletes were Terrell Davis, tailback for the Denver Broncos; Marcus Allen, running back for the Los Angeles Raiders and Kansas City Chiefs; and Ricky Williams, running back for the Miami Dolphins.

Of course, Reggie also cheered for his hometown team, the San Diego Chargers. His favorite pro team, though, was the San Francisco 49ers. He found it especially exciting to watch the interplay between quarterback Steve Young and wide receiver Jerry Rice, two of the team's legendary players, as Young threw touchdown after touchdown to Rice. In fact, Reggie was such a big fan of the 49ers that he even cheered them on when they won Super Bowl XXIX against the Chargers.

Besides playing football and studying its outstanding performers, Reggie gained valuable hands-on experience in other ways. At one point he had a chance to train with San Diego Chargers tailback LaDainian Tomlinson. In an article by Lee Jenkins in the *New York Times*, Tomlinson said about Reggie, "I noticed some of myself in him as far as creativity. He likes to express himself and do different things with the football."

The Early Years

Bush (*left*) studied the playing styles and training habits of famous football players to improve on his own game. One of these players, San Diego Chargers tailback LaDainian Tomlinson (*right*), recognized Bush's potential while leading a training camp for high school players.

Reggie also remembered Tomlinson well—mostly because of the toughness of their grueling workouts. Quoted in another article by Schrotenboer, Reggie recalled:

> It was the first time I ever threw up in a workout. I like to think of myself in pretty good shape, and he showed me what it takes. It's a whole other level. It changed my whole workout, my whole thought process, and I came back with a renewed focus.

Nonetheless, the young football player stuck with it. As Reggie reached his teen years, it seemed clear that he was headed toward an outstanding career playing high school ball.

Growing as an Athlete

Reggie Bush was already building a strong reputation when he started high school in 1999, at Helix High in nearby La Mesa. He was still tall but relatively slender, 5-foot-9 (1.75 m) and about 130 pounds (59 kg). Nonetheless, the staff of the Helix Highlanders football team thought they probably had a star in the making.

They were right. In his first scrimmage as a freshman, Reggie made a 60-yard run, and from that moment it was clear that he had tremendous potential. In a *New York Times* article by Lee Jenkins, Helix's principal, Doug Smith, said, "[I]t became apparent very early on that Reggie had a special feel for the game, a special sense of balance, an awareness of where he was on the field."

HIS SOPHOMORE YEAR

Football was not the only sport Reggie turned out for during his years at Helix. He was also an outstanding track athlete. For example, his 10.42-second time in the 100-meter dash set a state record—and he did it in his freshman year, wearing regular tennis shoes.

It was as a football player, though, that Reggie really stood out. Not surprisingly, he made the varsity team as a freshman. Like many freshmen players, however, he did not get a lot of time on the field.

As a sophomore, Reggie earned more playing time. He did this by starting to show what he was capable of doing. In one game, for instance, he ran for a score that officially measured 70 yards—although he juked and cut so often that several witnesses say it was more like 100. At the end of his sophomore season, the young athlete was named to the All-State team.

His high school career just got better. According to the Helix Highlanders' coach, Donnie Van Hook, on the first offensive play of Bush's junior season, the back caught a touchdown pass of 60-some yards from his teammate Alex Smith (who went on to a stellar career at the University of Utah and was the number one pick in the 2005 NFL Draft). Then, on the second offensive play, Bush threw a scoring pass of more than 60 yards. On the fourth play, he ran about 60 yards for a touchdown. (It is unclear why he was not involved in the third play as well.)

Reggie was building a reputation as a strong team player as well as an outstanding individual player. He never complained—not much, at least—about not getting enough touches in games. In an article by Austin Murphy in *Sports Illustrated*, Smith recalled, "There were times he might have been frustrated because he knew he could beat someone. But he wasn't the guy coming back to the huddle saying, 'I'm open! I'm open!'"

Bush joined quarterback Alex Smith (*above*) on the varsity football team in high school. Together, the two created a formidable offense for Helix High. Smith went on to become the top pick of the 2005 NFL Draft.

Off the field, the teen was earning a reputation as something of a fashion plate. Not even athletics could get in the way of his looking good, and Reggie was famous for always being one of the last players to leave the locker room. As Van Hook recalled in an article by Brent Schrotenboer, "[E]verything had to be perfect when he got dressed. If he ever was late to class, it's because he would just be slow getting dressed."

Another of Reggie's characteristics—on the field and off—was his quiet manner. Some classmates interpreted this as arrogance, but his coaches and teammates knew differently. They recognized that he was simply reserved and focused, instead of showing off or getting wild and crazy. Coach Van Hook said that Reggie was so calm and focused that a bomb could have gone off next to him and he would not have noticed.

INDUCING DIZZY SPELLS

Reggie was becoming increasingly vital to the Helix team, as reflected in the tremendous year he had as a junior—and the tremendous year the team as a whole had. Reggie finished the season with more than 3,000 all-purpose yards and 34 touchdowns, averaging 36 yards on each of his 28 touchdown rushes.

He was also a key element in the team's victorious postseason play. During the state semifinals, Reggie started off the fourth quarter with a touchdown run, then followed it with a touchdown pass and another touchdown run. Soon after, Reggie led the Highlanders to the state championship, and he was chosen as an All-State player.

Reggie was already known for his phenomenal speed, vision, toughness, and ability to outsmart his opponents. A good example is one play he made during his junior year, in a game against Monte Vista High School. He made a 32-yard run, during which he was nearly tackled for a five-yard loss, was hit or grabbed by defenders six times, nearly fell twice—and still scored a touchdown.

The Helix coaches also used Reggie to punt, trusting him to take advantage of the situation when he saw an opening. Many people who watched him in those days remember that it seemed as if Helix faked about as many punts as it attempted.

Kennedy Pola, formerly a running back coach at USC, where Reggie would soon play, was one of these observers. Quoted in the Jenkins article, Pola recalled, "Reggie would line up back there and make 22 people miss. That's 11 twice."

Helix's athletic director, Damon Chase, keeps videotapes of some of Reggie's best high school performances. In the *New York Times*, Jenkins wrote that this footage of Reggie's cutbacks, jump stops, spin moves, and slipped tackles "can induce dizzy spells, even for a jaded viewer numbed by hours of cable highlight shows."

"WHAT ELSE DO YOU NEED TO KNOW?"

Despite his stellar performances, however, Reggie was sometimes full of doubt about whether he wanted to continue to play. He sometimes felt as if people were constantly tugging at him and expecting too much. Playing football was not always as fun as it had been once.

In fact, at one point Reggie seriously considered quitting the game. Fortunately for his fans, his stepfather talked him out of it. LaMar told him that it did not matter what other people thought or expected. He counseled Reggie to instead play for God and for himself—and for no one else.

LaMar continued to counsel his son during these years. In these talks, LaMar stressed the importance of having humility, working hard in practice, and showing opponents respect. Perhaps most of all, LaMar stressed staying out of trouble. As reported by Wharton, LaMar recalled, "You have to make a decision in your life. You want to set yourself apart? You've got to do things the right way. I told him [that] over and over."

Reggie did not just excel on the field. The highly motivated athlete was also a highly motivated student, maintaining a

3.8 grade-point average. Furthermore, he was known to work harder than anyone else in the weight room.

This commitment is illustrated by an incident that happened early one morning during the summer between Reggie's junior and senior years. Coach Van Hook heard someone pumping iron in the school's weight room at 5:30 in the morning, two days before the start of practice. He discovered that Reggie had snuck in to work out by climbing on a bike rack and opening a window. Van Hook commented in a *Sports Illustrated* article by Austin Murphy:

> I said, "Reggie, what are you doing here?" He said, "Doesn't practice start today?" Here he is, a senior, getting recruited by everyone in the country, climbing in a window 10 feet off the ground in the dark so he can lift weights before practice. What else do you need to know about the kid?

REGGIE'S SENIOR YEAR

Reggie's senior year was as impressive as the rest of his time at Helix. He helped lead the Highlanders again to the California Interscholastic Federation (CIF) San Diego section Division II Championship Game. It was held at Qualcomm Stadium in San Diego. The Highlanders, though, lost to their longtime rivals, the Oceanside Pirates.

Meanwhile, Reggie racked up some serious statistics and honors for himself. Despite missing four games because of a broken wrist, he still rushed for 1,691 yards on 140 carries for an average of 12.1 yards and 27 touchdowns. *Parade* magazine put him on its prestigious All-American list, and *USA Today* named him All-USA. Furthermore, he was part of the U.S. Army's High School All-American team and took part in the All-American Bowl.

Overall, Reggie's high school career had soared. Not all of his games were victories, however. The most poignant instance came in his final high school game, when Oceanside upset Helix in the play-offs.

Reggie ran so hard during the game that he collapsed with cramps. He had to be treated with a saline solution delivered with an intravenous needle in his arm. The treatment helped get Reggie close to normal, but he was still not completely well. Nonetheless, he pleaded with his coaches to let him stay with his team rather than go home or to a hospital. At the end of the crushing defeat, he remained slumped in the locker room, ill and depressed. Even so, he still wanted to ride the bus home with his fellow Highlanders.

RECRUITED

Not surprisingly, a number of colleges strongly recruited Reggie as he neared the end of his high school career. Among them were such powerhouse programs as Notre Dame, Texas, Stanford, and the other Pac-10 schools.

One coach who was keenly interested was Rick Neuheisel, who was then the skipper of the University of Washington Huskies. In an article by Schrotenboer, Neuheisel recalled, "Reggie Bush was a phenomenal, I mean phenomenal talent on high school tape."

GOOD COMPANY

As an outstanding athlete at Helix High School, Reggie was in good company. A number of legendary sports figures are Helix alumni. Among them are center Bill Walton (basketball); wide receiver Todd Watkins (football); and linebacker Leon White (football). Furthermore, his high school teammate Alex Smith, now a quarterback for the San Francisco 49ers, was selected number one in the 2005 NFL Draft.

Also seriously interested in the senior was the football program at the University of Southern California in Los Angeles. Former USC fullback Kennedy Pola, who was the team's running back coach at the time, said that his colleagues were sold on Reggie when they saw his tape. In Jenkins's article in the *New York Times*, Pola commented, "That's the film that convinced the rest of the staff. They popped it in and went, 'Wow, we've got to get this guy.'"

Nonetheless, the University of Southern California Trojans were originally not even on Reggie's list of teams to consider. At first, Reggie was leaning heavily toward signing with Tyrone Willingham's team at Notre Dame. In the end, however, he decided that South Bend, Indiana, was too cold and too far from home.

Meanwhile, LaMar and Denise Griffin were carefully following the progress of their son's career to make sure he made the best decision. They wanted to be careful not to let the young man be influenced to make commitments he would later regret. Reggie's stepfather commented:

> It has to be done the family way. You're coming after us for our son. You've got to know up front that the family, we run the show. You call me. I'll get to you when I make the time to get to you. Agents and advisers will work around my schedule. I'm not being mean, but if you don't do that, some will take advantage of your time. I still have a job. I'm a husband, a father and a minister. I'm thinking about Reggie, and his time is really scarce. We have to make time and do what needs to be done for the family.

Reggie's parents supported the idea that he should check out USC more carefully. When he visited the school, Reggie liked what he saw. He had dinner with quarterback Matt Leinart, and they hit it off. The prospective Trojan also liked the hard work that USC put into practice, and he was attracted by the prospect of being able to go out for track there. (As it turned out, Reggie didn't pursue track. He chose to concentrate on football instead.)

The tailback also liked how frank the coaches were with him. They told Reggie honestly that he probably would not be a starter right away. In a 2005 article by Austin Murphy in *Sports illustrated*, Reggie said that the staff "kept it real. They didn't make all the promises in the world. They weren't blowing smoke."

"TAILBACK U"

Bush slowly began to change his mind in favor of USC. His parents supported this, feeling that he would fit in well there. In the end, he did choose USC—and he did fit in, but not at first. In high school he had been a major star, but in college he was just part of a crowd. When Bush arrived in the fall of 2003 and was assigned the number 5, he was one among many gifted players—in particular, talented offensive players—and it took some time before he adjusted.

One teammate was LenDale White, another promising freshman tailback. Their relationship could have turned into an ugly rivalry; it did not, however, because Bush and White got along well. White commented in Wharton's article, "We had to be friends. If we weren't, it would never have worked out."

The school had an especially strong reputation for fostering remarkable backs. John McKay, the university's legendary coach from 1960 to 1975, had developed a strategy that emphasized the position's importance. Under McKay and his successors, including John Robinson and Pete Carroll, the program turned out a number of outstanding players in that position.

There were so many of them that USC was given the nickname "Tailback U." But Bush was already from "Tailback Town," as some football fans had started to call San Diego. Among the Heisman Trophy winners from his hometown were

Marcus Allen (later of the Oakland Raiders and the Kansas City Chiefs), Ricky Williams (who went on to the Miami Dolphins and other teams), and Rashaan Salaam (who played for the Chicago Bears and several other teams).

Bush was keenly aware of this heritage. In Jenkins's article, he commented, "It means a lot to be from the same place as all those Heisman winners. That is something that really drives me.... I'm still curious to see if I can uphold the tradition."

WORKING ON HIS SKILLS

No one questioned the back's talents—especially his balance, agility, and blinding speed. His opponents were as aware of Bush's skills as anyone. One such opponent was Washington State linebacker Pat Bennett, who commented in Wharton's *Los Angeles Times* article, "He has that speed to where, even if you think you have him, he can give you a little juke and he's gone."

Nonetheless, Bush worked hard from the start to improve his natural athleticism. One reason for this was that his relatively small size raised questions among some observers. He was barely 6 feet tall and weighed 200 pounds, putting him in the middle range of the Trojans' backs in terms of size.

Bush was determined to be considered more than a lightweight. To this end, one skill he worked to perfect was to take the play in an unexpected direction. A play set up for "red return or right return" might end up as what his teammates and coaches called, "return right, Reggie left."

Bush's fellow Trojan, linebacker Dallas Sartz, who blocked for Bush on punt returns, said that anticipating Bush's direction was an exhilarating exercise. In Murphy's *Sports Illustrated* article, Sartz said, "It may throw us off ... but you've got to figure it's going to throw off the other team more. The thing with Reggie is, he's never going to give up on the play, so we can't either."

Bush's coach, Pete Carroll, said that even when it appeared that the back could not hurt an opponent, he probably would.

Murphy's *Sports Illustrated* article has the admiring coach commenting, "He's such a dynamic force that you have to know where he is, whether he's getting the ball or not. You have to watch him and do something about him."

FRESHMAN SEASON

Bush earned playing time from the start with the Trojans, mostly on special teams as a return man. It became increasingly clear to Carroll, however, that the freshman needed to get the ball more often. He was simply too good to keep in hiding, and he had definitely made his presence known.

During his freshman year, Bush rushed for 521 yards, averaging 5.8 yards on 90 carries. He gained another 492 yards returning kickoffs and was the first Trojan to lead the Pac-10 in kickoff returns since Anthony Davis in 1974. He also caught 15 passes for 314 yards and scored eight touchdowns (three rushing, four receiving, and one kickoff return). The 1,331 total yards he racked up were the most ever by a freshman in USC history.

Equally impressive was his fellow freshman LenDale White, whose 754 rushing yards led the team in that category. The main difference between the two lay in how they were used. Bush was a multi-threat weapon, while White mostly worked between the tackles. Trading off duties, they were becoming a formidable pair. Bush secured a number of honors at the year's end. He was a consensus Freshman All-American first-team selection and was named ESPN's Pac-10 Newcomer of the Year. USC had a stellar year, as well, finishing with a 12–1 record. The Trojans were named the national champions in the Associated Press poll.

A STERLING SOPHOMORE YEAR

Of course, Bush's life included more than football. Off the field, he continued to pursue his studies, majoring in political science. As in his high school days, friends and teammates described him as generally quiet, calm, and serious. He enjoyed relaxing like many other students his age, playing video games and watching movies. His romantic life during this period included dating future World Wrestling Entertainment (WWE) diva Eve Torres, who was then a student at USC.

During his sophomore year, Bush continued his streak. USC had another remarkable season, ending 12–0 and winning the Orange Bowl (pummeling undefeated Oklahoma by the lopsided score of 55–19.) Two other teams—Auburn and Utah—also ended the regular season undefeated, but it was clear which team deserved the national title.

Bush did his part in putting together the championship season. In the eyes of many observers, he was the most exciting player to emerge in college football during the early years of the new century.

A good example of how he played came during the Trojans' final regular-season game on December 4, 2004, against crosstown rivals UCLA. In that battle, Bush ran 15 times for 204 yards and scored on runs of 65 and 81 yards. Bush also led all receivers, racking up six catches for 73 yards, and he returned two kickoffs for 39 yards and two punts for 19 yards.

Bush did not start any game in 2004, but he nonetheless put together an impressive record. He had 143 carries for 908 yards and six touchdowns, adding on 509 yards and seven scores on 43 receptions.

Furthermore, Bush returned 21 kickoffs for 537 yards and 24 punts for 376 yards, plus a pair of touchdowns. His total all-purpose yardage, 2,330, made him the first Trojan to lead the Pac-10 in that category since Marcus Allen in 1981—and that was despite splitting time with LenDale White. He was also the first Trojan ever to win Pac-10 titles in both punt and kickoff returns.

As a result, the honors poured in. Included among the many he was given: He finished fifth in the Heisman Trophy contest, earned consensus All-American honors, and was a finalist for

Although Bush did not start in any games in the 2004 college football season for the University of Southern California, he was fifth in the voting for the Heisman Trophy. His teammate, Matt Leinart, won the prestigious award that year.

the Walter Camp Player of the Year Award. The Touchdown Club of Columbus selected him as the 2004 College Player of the Year. Football coaches, Cingular/ABC Sports, the *Sporting News,* ESPN.com, CSTV, AP, SI.com, and Rivals.com all named him to their 2004 All-American first teams.

As a capper, his teammates voted the athlete as the Trojans' Most Valuable Player. Quarterback Matt Leinart, who won the Heisman Trophy that year, was one of the many who appreciated his teammate's abilities. During a press conference on December 31, reprinted on a Web site maintained by the Orange Bowl Championship Committee, Leinart remarked:

> I voted for him. . . . It's a cool award because your teammates recognize who they believe [deserves it]. I got to

win that award last year. I've said all along that he's the best player in college football. He's so young, and it's tough.

With all of the players that we have, he probably doesn't get as many touches as he should get. But, he's a very unselfish player. That's why he's so good and such a great person. . . . I didn't even hesitate. I put his name right down. Obviously, the whole team felt the same way. He's impacted our team in a lot of different ways.

And that was just Bush's sophomore year. There would be many more accolades to come.

From College to the Pros

When the fall of 2005 rolled around, the Trojans were poised to continue to be as powerful a machine as the year before. In an article by *San Francisco Chronicle* writer Jake Curtis, Oregon Ducks coach Mike Bellotti remarked about coach Pete Carroll's talented players that year, "They're arguably one of the best offensive lines, not just in the nation, but in the history of college football."

Naturally, Carroll was thrilled to have Reggie Bush back for another season. The athlete, now in his junior year, was firmly on track to reprise his role as a key part of this remarkable lineup. One indication of Bush's promising future was that LaMar Griffin took out a $6 million insurance policy on his son. Griffin knew that Bush was likely to be drafted into the pros, either at the end of his junior year or after finishing college. The insurance policy would cushion the athlete financially in case he suffered a career-threatening injury.

THE TROJANS AND THE FIGHTING IRISH

As expected, all of USC's games during 2005 were exciting. The most memorable of these contests—and a defining moment in football history—was a victory on October 15 over USC's longtime rival, Notre Dame. The game took place in South Bend, Indiana, the home turf of Notre Dame's Fighting Irish.

Notre Dame had been doing well that season and was ranked ninth. USC, however, was doing even better. The Trojans were ranked first in the nation and were on a mind-boggling 27-game winning streak. And in the previous three seasons, they had three big wins over the Irish.

It was, without a doubt, the college football game of the year, and fans around the country were thrilled at the matchup. In the hype leading up to the contest, phrases like "game of the century" were freely tossed around. On the day of the game, an estimated 30 million households tuned in to see it, making it the most-watched regular-season college football game in nine years.

The first quarter started off slowly—until Bush struck with a 36-yard touchdown run. After that, the action heated up and the quarter ended with the Trojans leading 14–7. With the Irish pushing back, the second quarter saw the score flip-flop. At the half, the Irish were leading 21–14. Bush had the only scoring play in the third quarter, a 45-yard touchdown run, and in the fourth quarter Notre Dame placekicker D.J. Fitzpatrick made a 32-yard field goal, bringing the score to 24–21 with five minutes left in the game.

Then Bush ran for a 9-yard touchdown to complete an 80-yard drive led by quarterback Matt Leinart, giving the Trojans a 28–24 lead. With a little more than two minutes remaining, however, the Irish took the lead back: Quarterback

Bush's performance made the USC Trojans the team to watch during the 2005 college football season. In a game against longtime rivals Notre Dame, Bush dodged defensive players and ran 36 yards to score a touchdown.

Brady Quinn completed four passes for 53 yards, running back Darius Walker ran for 29 yards, and Quinn ran five yards for a touchdown. The game now stood at 31–28.

A FALSE END

Then the game got *really* interesting. After an incomplete pass, Leinart was sacked for a loss of 10 yards with 1:44 on the clock. The quarterback, though, was able to complete a 12-yard pass to Bush. The Trojans had fourth down and nine on their own 26-yard line. One minute and thirty seconds remained.

In the face of almost certain disaster, Leinart kept his cool. When he decided to change the play, the quarterback had to use hand signals—the roaring capacity crowd of 80,795 made it impossible for the players to hear anything. Leinart's plan was to deliver a pass to wide receiver Dwayne Jarrett, which both athletes perfectly executed. Jarrett went on to a 61-yard run before he was stopped on Notre Dame's 13-yard line.

Two rushes by Bush brought the Trojans to first-and-goal at the 2-yard line. Leinart scrambled toward the sideline, but Notre Dame linebacker Corey Mays knocked the ball out of bounds with a monstrous hit. Time was stopped on the field with seven seconds remaining.

But there was a problem. The timekeeper controlling the scoreboard let the clock run. Ecstatic Irish fans counted down the last seconds, thinking the game was truly ending. When the scoreboard clock ran out, the Notre Dame fans assumed that their team was victorious and began to rush the field. The game wasn't over, though, and the crowd had to be hastily herded back into the stands so that play could resume.

Seven seconds were put back on the clock—enough time for one more play. This play was not just crucial to the outcome of the game; it was also crucial to the Trojans' hopes for a victorious season. As it turned out, it was also a play that instantly became one of college football's greatest moments.

THE BUSH PUSH

Coach Carroll instructed Leinart to go for the touchdown with a sneak, rather than trying a field goal that would have tied the game and led to overtime. The quarterback agreed. When the Trojans got back to the line of scrimmage, they had a few moments before the referee signaled for play to begin.

There was enough time for Leinart to ponder the risky move and ask for Bush's opinion. Bush told him to go for it. In a *Sports Illustrated* article from December 2005 by Austin Murphy, Bush concisely summed up what came next: "He did, and it was as simple as that."

Leinart tried to sneak into the end zone. Stopped at the goal line by a daunting mass of Notre Dame players, he managed to bounce off the pile with his back to the goal. Bush then reached out and, with both hands on the quarterback's trunk, pushed him into the end zone—with three seconds on the clock.

Pandemonium ensued, resulting in a 15-yard penalty against USC for excessive celebration as the Trojans went wild with joy. This stunning development was followed by a missed extra point and Notre Dame's unsuccessful attempt at a kickoff return. The game ended with the Trojans victorious, 34–31.

"I DEFINITELY GAVE HIM A GOOD ENOUGH PUSH"

In the aftermath of this startling victory, the Irish dropped to 4–2 for the season and fell three places to twelfth in the national rankings. Meanwhile, the Trojans were now 6–0 with a 28-game winning streak and remained first in the rankings. And it happened because of the Bush Push, as the dazzling play was instantly dubbed.

The Bush Push is now generally considered to be one of college football's greatest moments. However, it has also been roundly criticized. Many observers have pointed out that the move was technically illegal. The NCAA rulebook specifically

From College to the Pros

In the last few moments in a game against Notre Dame, USC decided to go for a touchdown. As quarterback Matt Leinart (11) tried to get past the Notre Dame defense, Bush (5) shoved Leinart into the end zone, resulting in a touchdown.

forbids players from helping a ball carrier advance play by pushing, grasping, lifting, or charging.

If this infraction had been called, it would have resulted in a five-yard penalty and another play. For better or worse, it was not called. The Notre Dame coach, Charlie Weis, was understandably upset. Later, however, Weis acknowledged that he hoped his running back would have done the same thing in that situation.

For his part, Bush has always been cautious about discussing how crucial his part really was in the victory. At least in public, he has never taken much credit for the play's outcome. In Murphy's *Sports Illustrated* piece, the running back recalled, "It happened so quick. I'll never know if it really helped or it didn't. I definitely gave him a good enough push, though."

TRICK OR TREAT!

Naturally, the victory over Notre Dame helped the USC team bond even more than it already had. About two weeks after that game, Coach Carroll provided another team-building event, when he arranged an elaborate Halloween hoax.

Carroll had long been famous for playing elaborate practical jokes on his players, including one April Fool's Day trick in which members of the Los Angeles Police Department burst into a team meeting and pretended to arrest defensive end Everson Griffen for "physically abusing" a freshman. No one was sure if the arrest was real until Carroll showed a video of the "abuse"—Griffen knocking offensive guard Matt Meyer on his back during a routine drill.

The hoax Carroll organized at Halloween started during practice. LenDale White got into a yelling match with Carroll and offensive coordinator Lane Kiffin. White claimed that he was furious that he was not getting enough carries.

Only a few coaches and players knew that White's anger was prearranged. White was apparently quite convincing. Kiffin was not in on the joke, and he ordered White to leave practice. White replied that he quit and left.

Practice resumed and Carroll told his team that it could win even without White. Then the Trojans heard White shouting from the top of a building, yelling that he hated football. The next thing they knew, a body with a number 21 jersey fell from the roof of the building.

It was a dummy, of course, and at this point the team realized that it was a joke. It came out later that Bush was one of the few who had known of the hoax beforehand. In fact, Carroll had asked him to play White's role. The coach, however, told reporters that Bush got cold feet: "Reggie was scared to go on the roof so he talked LenDale into it."

AND THE WINNER IS . . .

When the 2005 season ended, Bush was the clear front-runner for the Heisman Trophy. Few were surprised that Bush was the favorite to win. In a *Sports Illustrated* article in November, writer Arash Markazi wryly noted, "Anyone who has watched what Bush has done this season understands the race is already over. The only intrigue left is what trendy nightclub Matt Leinart and Bush will go to after the ceremony and how many of their celebrity friends will show up."

Publicly, Bush and Leinart both said that they were supporting the other for the award. When asked by writer Sean Gregory, in an article in *Time* magazine, if he had Leinart's vote, Bush replied, "I hope so. We joke around about it. It was all in the plan, get it to him last year and get it to me this year." Asked in the same article if he had the Heisman sewn up, Bush seemed philosophical about it: "I don't know. I've said the same thing all along. If it's my time to win it, I'll win it, no matter what happens."

As expected, though, Bush prevailed. He beat the other finalists, who included Leinart and Texas quarterback Vince Young, by a record margin (84.9 percent of the first-place votes and 91.7 percent of the total ballots). The back had 784 first-place votes, the second-highest figure in that category in the 71-year history of the Heisman.

With this award, Bush became the fourth running back who was raised in San Diego to win the Heisman. He was also the seventh USC player, and the fifth USC tailback, to receive it. Young came in second in the contest, with 79 first-place votes. As a result, he lost a bet with Bush. The two friends had agreed that whoever was not chosen would make an appearance on *The Best Damn Sports Show* wearing the other player's jersey.

"IT TAKES A MAN..."

At the ceremony honoring him on December 10, Bush looked as natty as always, dressed in a three-piece suit and diamond earrings. He was tearful and emotional during the ceremony—and he was so nervous that he forgot the words he had planned to use. Instead, he improvised a speech and simply spoke from his heart.

In this impromptu speech, he thanked his family, especially his father, for supporting him over the years. Quoted in an article by Brent Schrotenboer in the *San Diego Union-Tribune*, Bush remarked warmly about how LaMar Griffin had taken him in and raised him as his own. The athlete added, "It takes a man to do something like that."

Naturally, Bush's old coaches at Helix High were proud of their famous alumnus. Damon Chase, Bush's high school trainer (and, more recently, Helix's athletic director), commented in Schrotenboer's article, "It's pretty awesome. We're certainly very happy and excited to call Reggie one of our own. It's going to take awhile for it all to sink in."

MORE HONORS

The other honors Bush received for the season just completed were further indications of his dominance in college ball. He was a unanimous All-American first-team pick. He was also named the Associated Press's Player of the Year, the Pigskin Club of Washington D.C.'s Offensive Player of the Year, and the Touchdown Club of Columbus's Player of the Year.

Furthermore, he received the prestigious Walter Camp Player of the Year Award and the Doak Walker Award as the nation's best college running back. Bush, along with Leinart, also graced the cover of the December 25, 2005, issue of *Sports Illustrated*. The magazine called them the year's "Best in College Football."

From College to the Pros

In 2005, Bush was named the winner of the Heisman Trophy, the seventh USC player to receive this honor. He won by a record margin, with 91.7 percent of all the votes.

There was a lot of discussion among fans and in the media about where Bush stood compared to other outstanding Trojan backs of past years. When reporters asked him about it, Bush

(continues on page 50)

ELUDING A TACKLER IN A PHONE BOOTH

Some observers argue that Reggie Bush's greatest moments came during his college career. It seemed that every time he was on the field he would do something amazing. In this excerpt from a *Sports Illustrated* article, Austin Murphy describes one such game and quotes some of Bush's admirers:

The play starts with such promise for Charles Burnley. A gunner on Oregon State's punt coverage unit, he gets a great release off the line of scrimmage and beats his blocker. Booking down the field, he slices through the mist in Corvallis on this November 2004 night, his Beavers trailing Southern Cal by a point early in the fourth quarter. All week Burnley's coaches had hammered home the dangers presented by Trojans return man Reggie Bush, who at this moment is ranging far to his right to field a punt most players would let roll out-of-bounds.

Burnley is bearing down on Bush, has him pinned against the sideline and sized up for a zoo hit, a *SportsCenter*-caliber undressing. But it never happens. With the gunner four yards out and closing, Bush feints right—toward the sideline—but Burnley isn't buying. So Bush jukes toward the open field, and Burnley takes the bait. Then Bush spins back to the right, and the gunner whiffs, hurtling past the USC player, his arms outstretched like Superman.

Essentially, Bush has eluded a tackler in a phone booth, but he's still got trouble. Skirting the sideline, he is hemmed in by a half dozen Beavers. This time Bush reverses the order of his fakes—left, right, then an explosive move back to the outside, to daylight. This is the burst that wrong-foots his pursuers, buckling their knees, immersing them in some unseen Class III rapid that leaves them at war with their own momentum, reaching vainly upstream.

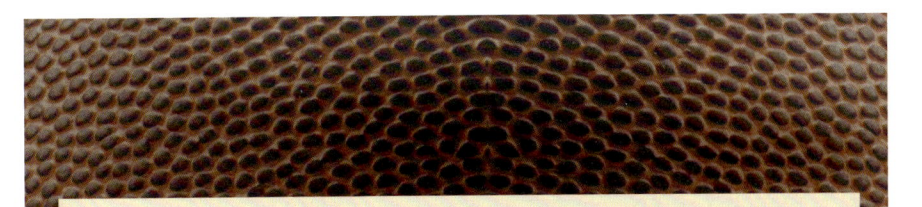

Bush makes those six moves in a space of five yards, in little more than two seconds. Seven seconds after that he is in the end zone, celebrating a 65-yard punt return. USC wins 28-20.

"Sometimes I go back and watch myself [on tape]," says Bush.... "To be honest, I'm not really conscious of what I'm doing while I'm doing it. Even after, I don't really remember what I did."

The Trojans' undefeated run to the national championship [in 2004] can be attributed in part to the Reggie Factor, which has corollaries that speak to the futility of trying to contain Bush—the first of which Burnley is now familiar with: Life isn't fair. You can do everything right, be in perfect position to stop him, and Bush will still hurt you.

"I think he's the best player in college football," says the best player in college football, USC quarterback and 2004 Heisman Trophy winner Matt Leinart, passing judgment on his teammate. "With his ability to change a game in one play, to make a defense look silly, to be a threat to score every time he touches the ball, there's no one else like him. He's the best."

"He's a tailback on one snap, a receiver on another," says Bob Gregory, defensive coordinator at Cal, the last team to beat USC, in September 2003. "They'll put him in the slot or motion him out of the backfield to try and get a mismatch."

"Bush can hurt you so many ways," says Arizona coach Mike Stoops. "You're more conscious of him than you are of Leinart."

Corollary II: Even when it looks like he's not in position to hurt you, he's probably going to hurt you. Says Trojans coach Pete Carroll, "He's such a dynamic force that you have to know where he is, whether he's getting the ball or not. You have to watch him and do something about him."

(continued from page 47)

replied that he was probably the worst person to ask. He added that he would be honored to be mentioned in the same breath as players like Marcus Allen, Bush's fellow San Diego native and Heisman winner.

Others were not as modest as Bush in their appraisal of his talents. The comments of Marcus Allen himself were typical of the praise being heaped on the young athlete. In a *San Diego Union-Tribune* article published at the time, Allen commented, "Now, only time will tell if he ends up as one of the greats to play the game. Certainly he's going to be considered one of the greatest college players of all time."

THE ROSE BOWL

USC had not done so badly as a team, either. The Trojans kept their winning streak alive for the entire season, remaining number one in the national rankings. And so, a few weeks after Bush's Heisman ceremony, the team headed to the Rose Bowl on January 4, 2006.

In the game, USC faced the second-ranked Texas Longhorns for the national championship. The two teams were well matched, although many commentators favored the Trojans, in large part because of their powerhouse offense. Adding to the excitement was the fact that Bush, the Heisman winner, was matched up against Young, the runner-up. The contest also marked the first time that two Heisman winners, Bush and Leinart, played in the same backfield.

During the game, Bush was well contained by the Longhorns and had to settle for a decent but not stellar performance. Overall, his play was overshadowed by the brilliant work of LenDale White and Vince Young. Perhaps Bush's most memorable move was a touchdown—his only one of the day—on a 26-yard run, bouncing an inside handoff to the outside and leaping from the 5-yard line into the end zone. In all he had

95 yards on just six catches, 102 kickoff return yards, and 82 yards on 13 carries for a total of 279 all-purpose yards.

All told, the Trojans put up a valiant fight, dominating the first half of the game. After some dramatic seesaw scoring, the underdog Longhorns prevailed 41–38—the first loss in a Rose Bowl for USC since 1989. In a measure of how close the game was, Texas's victory was secured only in the final 10 seconds. *Sports Illustrated* and *Time* singled out this remarkable game as the year's best sports moment, and many consider it one of the most memorable contests in all of college football.

Despite the bitter loss, the Rose Bowl capped an exceptional season for Bush. He ended with 2,890 all-purpose yards, the most ever by a USC player, and a total of 19 touchdowns. Besides his many other honors, Bush also ended the season ranked nationally in several categories: He was tenth for all-purpose yards per game, ninth for rushing yards per game, seventh for points scored, eighth for yards per punt return, and first for yards per carry.

GOING FOR THE DRAFT?

Fans and media pundits had been speculating all season about the possibility of Bush skipping his senior year to enter the NFL Draft. With two national championships under his belt and a raft of clearly proven skills, it appeared that this would be a natural progression.

As might be expected, the pros were keenly interested in him. Charles White, the 1979 Heisman-winning running back from USC, said that scouts were most impressed with Bush's speed, as well as his ability to cut on a moment's notice. White was one of many who compared Bush to Gale Sayers, another player who always seemed two steps faster than anybody else and made changing direction at full speed look easy.

Some observers were skeptical. They wondered about Bush's ability to handle the 25 or 30 touches per game that would be required of him in the pros. This was a minority opinion, however, and most of those involved—including Bush himself—dismissed it. As one scout, quoted in Markazi's *Sports Illustrated* article, commented, "He's a once in a lifetime player."

Publicly, Bush had remained noncommittal all season. Over and over, he told reporters that he would not make a decision until after the season. Three days before the Rose Bowl, in an article by Teddy Greenstein in the *Chicago Tribune*, Bush said:

> I was just talking about how the media has kind of made the decision for me, not given me the option. They've sort of told me I'm going pro. It's fine. Like I said all year, I won't make my decision until after this season. [But] the fact that I could be the No. 1 draft pick will obviously be a dream come true.

In fact, Bush did decide to pursue that dream. On January 12, 2006, he announced he would declare for the draft. That April, at USC's pro day, Bush—at 201 pounds (91 kg)—demonstrated his athleticism to scouts by bench-pressing 24 times with the 225-pound (102 kg) weights. He also ran the 40-yard (36.58 m) dash in 4.33 seconds, had a standing broad jump of 10-foot-9 (3.28 m), and a vertical leap of 40.5 inches (103 cm).

Soon after, in an interview with Richard Deitsch in *Sports Illustrated*, Bush said that he felt he had laid any lingering doubts to rest. He stated, "I think it was a productive day and I accomplished everything I wanted to. I felt I could have run a little faster, and maybe add[ed] one or two reps to the bench press. But I feel like I showed the scouts that I'm still going to perform like I have something to prove."

He soon would.

Going to New Orleans

The Houston Texans appeared to be extremely interested in obtaining Reggie Bush. It was widely speculated, and assumed by many, that the running back would be the team's choice for the first pick in the 2006 draft. On April 28, the day before the draft, however, the Texans announced that they had signed a deal with North Carolina State's defensive end Mario Williams.

This meant, of course, that Bush would not be the year's first draft pick. Although he might have been disappointed, the athlete was publicly gracious in his praise for Williams. Soon after the announcement, Bush commented to a reporter for IGN Sports, "Mario Williams is a great player. He's worked his behind off to get to this point like we all have. He's very deserving of being the No. 1 pick. I wish him the best and I hope he succeeds."

GOING TO NEW ORLEANS

Bush was philosophical about the decision. He acknowledged to reporters that it was out of his hands and that he was not insulted by the choice. The athlete pointed out that teams used their draft picks to choose certain players with specific skills, hoping to fill holes in their lineups. He told IGN Sports reporter Jonathan Miller:

> There was obviously a lot of speculation going on. Everybody thought I was going to Houston. For me, I just came into this process with an open mind. At the end of the day, it's still a business.
>
> We've [the players] done our part up to this point. We've done the pro days and the film and the tapes and we've done everything we can. At the end of the day, it's up to the teams. We have no control over this thing. It's up to the teams to choose who they feel is going to best suit their program.

Many analysts ridiculed Houston's decision to skip Bush as a major mistake. Nonetheless, there were plenty of other teams also interested in the back. Within hours, Internet chat rooms were buzzing with comments from excited fans about where he might go. Most of the speculation centered around the New York Jets and the San Francisco 49ers.

Bush liked the prospect of going to San Francisco, since he would have been reunited with his high school teammate Alex Smith. Furthermore, the 49ers had been his favorite team when he was a kid. In an article by Jake Curtis of the *San Francisco Chronicle*, Bush recalled, "I used to love watching the 49ers growing up—Young, Rice, Ricky Watters. They used to beat the mess out of teams. My dad and I loved watching them."

However, the New Orleans Saints announced their intention to use the second overall pick to choose Bush. The Saints, part of the South Division of the National Football Conference

(NFC), had been around since 1967. The franchise had been founded as part of an expansion move by the National Football League (NFL).

JOINING A STRUGGLING TEAM

The Saints had not had a terrific record over the years. In fact, the team had such a dismal record that discouraged fans took

> ### SMILES FOR THE FANS IN NEW ORLEANS
>
> Reggie Bush was happy with the outcome of the draft and seemed grateful for the opportunity to go to New Orleans. He was especially conscious of the good he could do by playing on behalf of a city that was rebuilding in the aftermath of a destructive hurricane. He told Jonathan Miller, a reporter for IGN Sports:
>
>> I'm just excited to be back on a football team. It's been a long time coming for all of us, everybody that was invited to this draft, we [all the draft picks] should all be appreciative I think for being in this position. There's a lot of guys that would kill to be in our shoes right now and this is a blessing to be here and for our families to be here to share this experience with us. . . .
>>
>> I feel like I could help possibly bring some smiles back to the faces of New Orleans. But . . . they have been through a lot, and . . . hopefully we can help turn this program around. Like I said, just bring some happiness back to the city and compete in the playoffs. I think we have a great chance of competing this year. They have got some great receivers, Deuce McAllister; Drew Brees they just added, so they have some weapons. I think we should be able to compete next year.

to wearing paper bags over their heads because they were so embarrassed. (Some fans decorated their bags with the word "Aints" instead of "Saints.")

The Saints spent more than a decade struggling before they even succeeded in finishing a season with a .500 record. It took two decades before the Saints even had a winning season.

Its first successful period stretched from 1987 to 1992. During this time, the team made the play-offs four times and had winning records in the non-play-off seasons. The team struggled again for a few more years, and then, at the end of the 2000 season, New Orleans defeated the defending Super Bowl champions, the St. Louis Rams, to earn their first play-off win. After that season, though, the Saints again failed to make the play-offs.

Now Reggie Bush would become a Saint. He was making his dream come true and becoming a professional football player. Not just that—he would be entering the pros as one of the hottest rookies chosen that year, a player with a sterling record and tremendous potential.

His salary reflected this promise. Later that year, in the summer, he signed a contract that would give him a potential $62 million over the next six years. (This figure included performance incentives.)

As a Saint, Bush would be joining, among others, quarterback Drew Brees, fellow running back Deuce McAllister, and the team's new coach, Sean Payton. (Meanwhile, the Jets used their pick to acquire offensive tackle D'Brickashaw Ferguson out of Virginia, while the 49ers opted for Maryland's tight end Vernon Davis.)

"BACK FLIPS AND HANDSTANDS"

The drafting of Bush was part of a major rebuilding effort by the Saints. This undertaking included bringing in 28 new players as well as the new coach. Payton had arrived in New Orleans after serving as an offensive assistant for the New York Giants and the Dallas Cowboys.

Going to New Orleans

The Houston Texans got first pick in the 2005 NFL Draft but passed on Bush in favor of Mario Williams. The San Francisco 49ers and the New York Jets were rumored to be interested in Bush, who ultimately headed to New Orleans to join the Saints.

He took over in January 2006 from Jim Haslett. In 2000 Haslett had led the Saints to their only play-off victory in four decades, but he was fired after a stretch that culminated in a 2005 season with only three wins. Fans hoped that Payton could rebuild and revitalize the struggling franchise.

It was clear that the Saints were delighted with the opportunity to make Bush part of their rebuilding effort. In turn, he said he was happy to be going somewhere that was so excited about him. In his interview with IGN Sports, Bush remarked:

> I talked to Coach Payton and he said that . . . when they [the Saints organization] found out I wasn't going to Houston, they threw all the draft cards in the air and they were doing back flips and handstands and all that. Any organization that's pumped up about me makes me feel good and want to go there and play.

Payton was not the only one to welcome the hotshot new recruit. The quarterback, Drew Brees, called Bush to say that he was pleased that the back would be playing for the Saints. Bush remarked later that he considered it a great compliment just for Brees to take the time to call.

The rookie also found support from running back Deuce McAllister. It might have been understandable if McAllister considered Bush a potential rival. According to Bush, however, McAllister displayed no jealousy. In an article by Arash Markazi, Bush said, "Deuce could have been offended by the fact that I was coming to his team. . . . But that's not Deuce. He took the time to explain things to me. Every single day he told me something to help me get through another day in pro football."

Meanwhile, the city's ecstatic Saints fans were not shy about welcoming Bush to their town. On his first trip there, word got out that he had been spotted in a certain local restaurant. A wide variety of residents—rich and poor, black and white—lined up outside the place, hoping just to catch a glimpse of Bush.

At the same time, there were other signs of interest in him. Ticket sales for the upcoming season hit record highs, and vendors all over the city were selling out of T-shirts sporting Bush's name and face. Furthermore, there was a massive rush to buy replicas of the athlete's jersey. Within a week of the draft, Reebok (the makers of the official jersey replicas) had received more than 15,000 orders—even though no one knew yet what Bush's number would be.

The people of New Orleans had good reason to feel joyful. Of course, they were simply excited by Bush's potential for rebuilding the Saints. This enthusiasm, though, was just one aspect of something far more important: the football player's symbolic role in helping to rebuild the city itself.

SAINT REGGIE

Less than a year before, in August 2005, New Orleans had experienced the worst disaster in its history—Hurricane Katrina, one of the deadliest storms on record in the United States.

Katrina killed thousands of people. Tens of thousands more were missing or left homeless. Large portions of the famed city and the area around it were destroyed. The region was left in chaos, and hope was in short supply.

The struggle to rebuild the city, mourn for the dead, and house or relocate homeless people was long and sad. The process was complicated by accusations of mismanagement and incompetence at virtually every level of government.

So the will, strength, heart, and stamina of the people of Louisiana were being sorely tested by the time the NFL Draft arrived in April. The hiring of a new coach and the acquisition of promising new players like Bush provided a small but important boost of morale, a sign that something was going right in a town where a great deal was going wrong. In fact, so much hope was riding on Bush that he was given another new nickname: "Saint Reggie."

In a *Sports Illustrated* article, writer Douglas Brinkley pointed out one reason Bush was becoming a hero to so many: He was accessible. In a town with too little money and too few resources, the athlete was someone everyone could relate to. Brinkley commented, "Cash-strapped New Orleans can't properly equip its high school football teams, but the poorest kid [can] afford to Scotch-tape a newspaper picture of [Bush] to the refrigerator."

BUILDING TEAMWORK

One mark of the city's sense of excitement and anticipation was the rush of crowds to Jackson, Mississippi, to watch Bush in action at preseason camp. (During camp, receiver Joe Horn gave the rookie another new nickname: "Baby Matrix." Bush's ability to outwit opponents reminded Horn of how people in the movie *The Matrix* impossibly evaded bullets.)

Payton ran an especially tough camp that, in part, emphasized the players' individual strengths. But the new coach also worked hard to demonstrate his belief that teamwork, not individual talent, was the key to success. Payton illustrated his point in a meeting during camp when he discussed the athletes who had made up the U.S. men's basketball team for the 2004 Olympics.

He noted that the most brilliant hoops players and coaches alive were brought together for the Olympic team, which then suffered a humiliating loss to Argentina. The Americans were a group of gifted individuals who had not been able to cohere as a single, effective unit. Payton's point was to emphasize the importance of valuing team discipline and chemistry over the virtues of specific players.

Another aspect of Payton's team-building strategy was to acknowledge the notorious party atmosphere of New Orleans. For scores of years, the city's reputation has been that of a casual, anything-goes place. In fact, the city's nickname is "the Big Easy."

Going to New Orleans   61

When Bush joined the Saints, the team had just acquired a new coach, Sean Payton. Determined to build a strong, successful team, Payton (*left*) designed a tough training camp that year to instill discipline in Bush and the other players.

For anyone susceptible to temptation, such a town could be full of pitfalls. The coach knew that he needed to instill in his players enough discipline to avoid the city's temptations. In a *Sports Illustrated* article by Michael Silver, Payton stated:

> You have to look at why they've only won one playoff game in 40 years. There's a reason. We're in a place where, within 10 minutes, you can get a daiquiri, sit at a blackjack table and go to a strip club—and you can do it

at four in the morning. If you've got the type of people on your team who are susceptible to that, they'll find trouble. So yeah, character's important.

DONATING TO RELIEF HELP

As he began to settle into life in New Orleans, Bush was clearly interested in returning some of the good feelings that the city was showing him. One way was to donate significant amounts of money to worthy causes. For example, he gave $50,000 to a private school for students with learning disabilities when the school was being threatened with closure. He also supplied funds to buy vehicles for a suburban police department.

Bush did more than donate his own money, however. He also recruited help from some of the companies that were signing him to endorsement deals. For example, he and the Adidas sportswear firm donated $86,000 to maintain a football field for high school players. Gold Toe socks, meanwhile, donated 100,000 pairs of its product to New Orleans charities.

The list went on. Schutt, a company that makes football gear, donated helmets and uniforms to a high school. Hummer donated 12 vehicles to government agencies. Two of Bush's other corporate sponsors, Pepsi and Subway, also pledged significant donations. And Bush was named a regional spokesman for the nonprofit Make-A-Wish Foundation, which helps seriously ill children fulfill their dreams.

"I WANTED TO GIVE SOMETHING BACK TO THEM"

Besides these and other donations, Bush took another important and well-publicized step. It began with the question about which number would appear on his jersey. Bush wanted to continue to wear number 5, which had been his number throughout high school and college. NFL regulations, however, state that running backs must wear numbers between 20 and 49.

As a compromise, Bush was allowed to wear number 5 temporarily during preseason practices. Meanwhile, he devised a plan. He promised that, if he could continue to wear number 5, he would donate 25 percent of his income from jersey sales to Hurricane Katrina victims. The NFL, however, ruled against Bush. The league instead gave him number 25. This number was inherited from running back Fred McAfee, who had just wrapped up his second stint with the Saints.

Bush was disappointed, but he announced that he would donate 25 percent of his jersey sales anyway. Half would go to McAfee's favorite charities, and half to Bush's. McAfee donated his portion to hurricane relief efforts in his native Mississippi, while Bush earmarked his for victims in New Orleans. In an interview with a British newspaper, the *Guardian*, Bush commented about his various acts of philanthropy:

> I thought it was important, as the city needs a lot of help. I wanted to be a part of that community that needed inspiration, with so many kids there, people who lost family members and who lost their property—they needed something positive.... They embraced me, I wanted to give something back to them.

"A LEARNING PROCESS"

Meanwhile, the team was getting ready for its real work: the 2006 schedule. The year before, during the 3–13 season that led to Haslett's dismissal, the team had not been able to play games in its home, the Superdome. Its preseason games in 2006 also had to be played out of town.

The changes in venue were necessary because the Superdome needed extensive repairs. The stadium had been at the very center of the chaotic efforts to bring aid to the city during Hurricane Katrina, and the structure was severely damaged. In 2005, the team played its opening "home" game against the New York Giants at Giants Stadium. The remainder of the

Saints' 2005 home games were held at the Alamodome in San Antonio, Texas, and Louisiana State University's Tiger Stadium in Baton Rouge.

Repairs to the Superdome cost some $185 million. Now, however, the Superdome was back in shape and ready for the Saints. This fact alone was reason for celebration and high expectations.

Meanwhile, Bush was working to make the transition from college ball to the much faster and more physical NFL style of football. In the *Guardian* interview, he said, "It has been tough. When you join the NFL you start from scratch. As long as I've been playing—which has been since I was eight years old—the game becomes harder at every level. . . . So it's been a learning process for me."

"IT WAS MAGICAL"

Despite his doubts, during his first preseason game, on August 12 against the Tennessee Titans, Bush stunned the crowd with his performance and with one spectacular move in particular. He swept to his left, ran into a swarm of Titans, turned back, shifted gears, and gained 44 yards. Bush later commented that he was the one who was really excited, since this game was his first in the pros. In the Markazi article, he recalled:

> I was totally jacked up. There was electricity in that stadium that I've never felt before. There were people crying, there were people laughing, there were people hugging [and] the players were just pumped. I've played in some really, really big games in my career, but never was there a feeling for me like there was the night of that opening game. It was magical.

The Saints beat the Titans but then lost the next three preseason games before launching a three-game winning streak at the start of the regular season. The first of these wins marked Bush's first regular-season pro game, a 19–14 away-game victory against the Cleveland Browns. Bush rushed for 67 yards—not as many as Deuce McAllister, however, ensuring that the older back would be the starter for the rest of the year. Payton chose to use Bush instead in special situations where he was most likely to succeed.

On September 25, Bush played in his first home game, against the Atlanta Falcons, before a sold-out crowd of 70,000. The game was also nationally televised on *Monday Night Football*. Attracting a viewership of nearly 11 million homes, the game was ESPN's highest-rated program to date. In fact, it was the second-highest-rated cable program of all time. Adding to the excitement were performances by two of the world's biggest rock bands. U2 and Green Day performed "Wake Me Up When September Ends" and "The Saints Are Coming" before the game.

The occasion was a sentimental homecoming party—the first game the Saints had played in the reopened and repaired Superdome—so it seemed appropriate that New Orleans thrashed the favored Falcons 23–3. The Saints' victory later received a 2007 ESPY award for "Best Moment in Sports."

Much more significant, however, was the game's symbolic importance, giving comfort—if just for a night—to a region still in need of it. In an interview in *Men's Fitness*, Bush recalled, "That night was about more than football. The level of intensity was higher than any game I've ever played in. Everyone was impacted."

THE BUSH-MCALLISTER DUO

Bush finished the midway point of the season with 46 receptions, the most by any running back in the NFL, but he failed to score until November 12 in a matchup with the Pittsburgh Steelers. The touchdown, his first in a pro game, came while scrambling on a reverse. It was a big day for Bush, one that the game's conclusion—a loss for the Saints, 38–31—could hardly dampen for the rookie.

As the season wore on, Coach Payton began to use McAllister and Bush in the backfield at the same time. This turned out to be a deadly combination; the less experienced Bush did not get the ball as much as McAllister, but their skills meshed perfectly.

Typically, McAllister was the runner and Bush was the receiver. Often, Bush essentially acted as a wide receiver. The two also ran a number of reverses in which Bush handed the ball off to McAllister—the idea being that Bush would lure defenders away from McAllister. In another instance, in a game against the Niners, quarterback Drew Brees faked a handoff to McAllister and tossed the ball to Bush, who easily scored.

One important result of the McAllister-Bush combination was that it opened up the passing game for Brees, who was coming off a shoulder injury but proving himself still a formidable presence. Adding to this combination were wide receivers Marques Colston and Joe Horn, giving the Saints one of pro ball's best offensive lineups.

No matter what play they ran, the running backs always had the same result in mind, and they learned to work together to make it happen. In an article by Dan Pompei for NBCSports.com, Payton said, "It's hard for a running back to be unselfish, but there aren't any two players who are more concerned with winning."

ON TO THE PLAY-OFFS

Bush continued to shine for the rest of the season. On December 3, in the game against San Francisco, he tied the Saints' single-game touchdown record, held by Horn, scoring four (three rushing, one receiving) in a 34–10 blowout. He also gained 168 total yards, sparking the Saints to the eighth win of their season.

A week later, Bush scored a 62-yard touchdown against the Cowboys in Dallas, contributing to the Saints' 42–17 victory. Another significant game came on December 24, when he scored a one-yard touchdown on a reverse against the New York Giants. In this game, in which the Saints trampled the Giants 30–7, Bush carried the ball 20 times for 126 yards. It was, by far, his best rushing game of the season.

Of course, not all of his games were as exceptional. For example, a week before the Giants game, he ran for only 14 yards on seven carries in a loss to Washington. Also, in the last matchup of the regular season, a home game on December 31 against the Carolina Panthers, Bush scored a one-yard touchdown—but he also carried the ball just three times.

Despite these disappointments, the rookie's overall performance was encouraging. Playing in all 16 games, he finished with 565 rushing yards, 6 rushing touchdowns, 88 receptions, 742 receiving yards, and 2 receiving touchdowns. Furthermore, the Saints finished 10–6 and were headed to the play-offs for the first time since 2000. Bush had played a big part in this achievement.

BLOWN UP

The Saints' first play-off game, in the divisional round, was held on January 13, 2007, in the Superdome. The Saints edged the Philadelphia Eagles 27–24, thus earning the franchise its first NFC Championship Game appearance in its 40-year history. Bush had a good game personally as well: He ran for 52 yards on 12 carries, scored a touchdown, and added three catches for 22 yards.

On the other hand, in what appeared on film to be a carefully choreographed move, Eagles cornerback Sheldon Brown landed a vicious hit on Bush (although he escaped serious injury). Brown flew through the air with his arms extended, driving his right shoulder into Bush's chest and stomach. The impact lifted the back into the air and carried him backward three yards. The two players' bodies flew together until Bush's back slammed into the turf and the ball bounced away. Bush's elbow was pinned against his body, which protected his rib cage and probably kept his ribs from breaking.

The New Orleans crowd, which had been in a fever-pitch frenzy only seconds before, fell silent as it waited for Bush to get up. Bush rose quickly to his hands and knees, then to one knee before standing up. And then he fell back on all fours, pawing at the ground and trying to get his wind back. *Sports Illustrated* writer Tim Layden commented, "Bush was on his hands and knees on the turf of the Louisiana Superdome, crawling in his black New Orleans Saints uniform like a small child, sent back to his infancy after getting blown up by Eagles cornerback Sheldon Brown."

It was a situation Bush was definitely not used to. He had always been the best athlete on the field in high school and college, too fast and slippery to leave himself open. In this case, however, he received a hard lesson in how the game is played NFL style. The moment was so dramatic that it made the cover of *Sports Illustrated*.

"IT WAS STUPID"

It had been more than unlikely at the beginning of the season, but the Saints were now in an NFC Championship Game. Facing the Chicago Bears in the snow on the Bears' home turf, New Orleans struggled at first. Then the game took a turn; the Saints seemed set for a second-half comeback after Bush took a pass from Brees on the 12-yard line and dashed 88 yards for a breathtaking touchdown, trimming Chicago's lead to 16–14.

Bush, though, made an immature mistake on this play. When it became clear that he was going to score, he turned and waved a finger mockingly at linebacker Brian Urlacher and the other Bears who were in hot pursuit. Then Bush did a somersault into the end zone and a little victory dance. The NFL fined Bush $5,000 for his conduct, despite the athlete's immediate apology.

Going to New Orleans

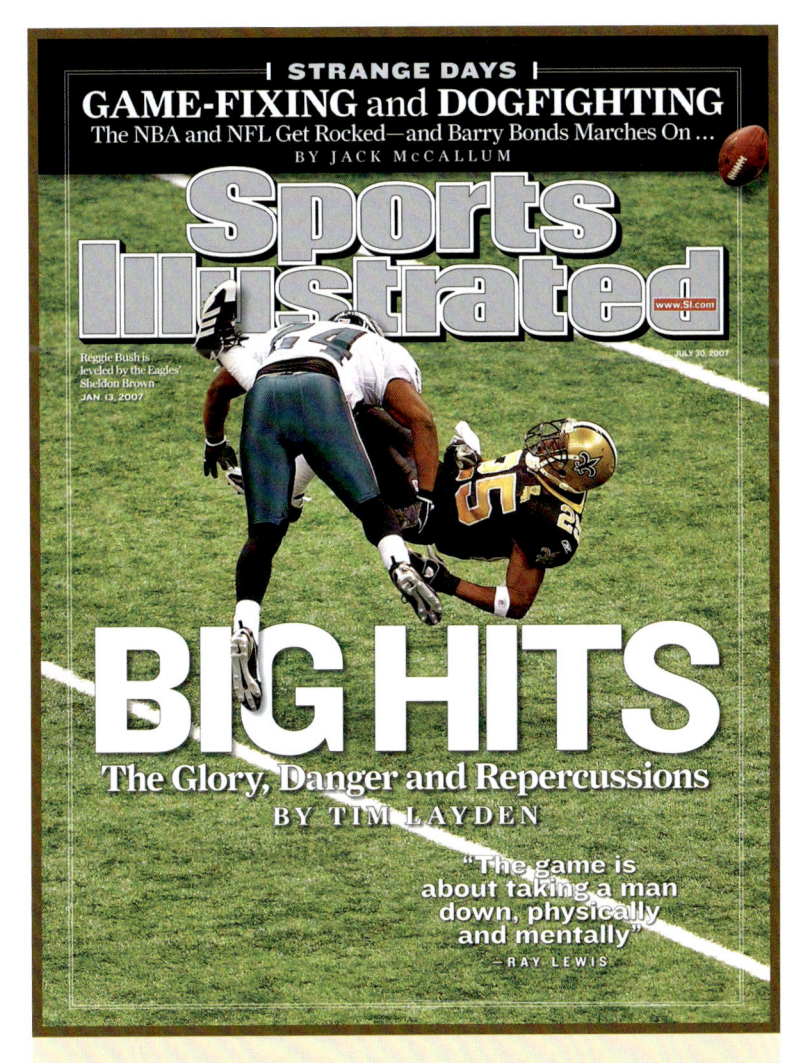

In Bush's first season playing professional football, he received an incredible hit from Eagles player Sheldon Brown. Brown hit Bush so hard, both players became airborne and moved three yards.

The money was nothing to someone as wealthy as Bush, but he did come in for criticism from many quarters. The back defended his actions by saying he simply got caught up in the emotion of the moment. In the *Men's Fitness* article, he said, "It was stupid, I'm sorry, and I'll never do it again. If that's the worst mistake I'll make as a pro, then I'll be OK. When the Chicago Bears went to sleep that night, I think it was the last thing they were thinking about."

END OF THE SEASON

Perhaps the Bears were not thinking about Bush's stunt when they went to sleep because they were victorious that day, cruising to a 39–14 victory. With this, the Bears were headed to the Super Bowl and the Saints ended their season with an overall record of 11–7.

Despite the bitter loss, New Orleans's winning ways proved to be football's feel-good story of 2006. As for Urlacher, he said he didn't mind that Bush acted in an unsportsmanlike way—all he cared about was that the Bears won that day. In an article in the *Chicago Tribune*, the linebacker said:

> I think we won that game, right? Honestly, to me, that other stuff was so blown out of proportion. I don't think Reggie directed that toward me. I don't even think about it until somebody brings it up. He was excited about his play and turned around and pointed, I guess. And I was the guy right there. He's lucky I didn't catch him. If I was running at full speed, I would have.

The season also ended well for Bush. He came in fifth in the voting for Associated Press NFL Offensive Rookie of the Year. Bush also showed that he was fully capable of moving on to even better performances.

The 2007 and 2008 Seasons

For the second year in a row, the Saints sold out all of their games before the 2007 season began (even though the city had shrunk by hundreds of thousands of residents after the hurricane). The year was also a busy one for Bush. He bought a $5 million house in the Hollywood Hills section of Los Angeles, and he appeared often in the public eye. He also bought a house in New Orleans.

One reason for this exposure was that he picked up several more lucrative endorsement and advertising contracts. For example, he was the cover athlete for *Reggie Bush Pro Football 2007*, released by Gameloft, a French publisher of mobile games. He was also the cover athlete for Electronic Arts' *NCAA Football '07* game. And he signed a deal with Sirius Satellite radio to be a weekly sports announcer.

Furthermore, he appeared in a popular series of commercials with David Beckham, a superstar in the world of soccer, or football, as most of the world calls it. Bush and Beckham, who was then playing for the Real Madrid team in Spain, were featured in a 13-part video series sponsored by the Adidas sportswear manufacturer.

The series was called "*Futbol* Meets Football." (*Futbol* is the Spanish word for football.) In the commercials, Bush and Beckham humorously looked at the differences and similarities between the two sports while trying to teach each other the basics of their specialties.

IN THE PUBLIC EYE

Bush was often in the public eye in other ways as well. For example, he dined with Secretary of State Condoleezza Rice at a White House correspondents dinner. He was spotted in Las Vegas during the NBA All-Star weekend. He partied at the Playboy Mansion and numerous other places.

He also appeared in a video accompanying Ciara's song "Like a Boy." This sparked rumors of a romance between the two, although the reports were indeed nothing but rumors.

During this period, however, Bush did become involved in a serious and real-life romance. In the spring of 2007, the news broke that Bush was dating "celebutante" Kim Kardashian. The glamorous Kardashian was best known for her social life and for starring in a reality TV show, *Keeping Up with the Kardashians*. The two were introduced by a pair of mutual friends who were dating at the time: celebutante Paris Hilton and Matt Leinart, Bush's former teammate at USC.

Kardashian told a reporter that it took a while before Bush could work up the courage to ask for her phone number. Even then, the couple's first date was not exactly glamorous. In a *USA Today* article, Kardashian recalled, "We went to Chipotle and the car wash. I picked him up from the car wash and then we ate at Chipotle. Very sexy."

Beyond their romance, there was another interesting connection between Bush and Kardashian. Her late father, Robert Kardashian, was a manager of the USC football team before Bush played there. At the time, another Heisman-winning running back, O.J. Simpson, was a star for the Trojans. Robert Kardashian later became a lawyer and was part of Simpson's defense team during the famous football player's murder trial.

As his fame grew and attention increasingly focused on him, Bush developed a reputation for disliking interviews. He often said that he wished he had more privacy in his life. The paparazzi who constantly followed him were intensely annoying. In an interview with SI.com, Kardashian stated, "He hates the paparazzi, but he's such a big part of my life that you can't not be on [my] show if you're in my life.... We try to be super low key. We know if we go to an event, we're gonna be photographed, but he'll still say, 'Ugh, I don't want to go.'"

Nonetheless, Bush acknowledged that being famous had its advantages. For example, his celebrity meant that more people listened to him when he had something important to say. In an article by Brett Martel in the *St. Louis Post–Dispatch,* Bush said, "I welcome the celebrity with open arms because I feel like I can use that to make a difference in people's lives."

During this period, the back also spent a lot of time with one of his best friends, running back Adrian Peterson of the Minnesota Vikings—at least as much time as possible given their busy schedules.

On the field, however, the two had very different playing styles. Peterson tended to do his best work inside, while Bush preferred to spend his time in space—that is, out on the perimeter. No matter what their styles were, though, when Bush and Peterson faced each other on the field they acted as any competitive athletes would, temporarily putting their friendship aside.

Despite their different ways of playing, the two stars respected and admired each other's styles. In an article by Chip Scoggins in the *Minneapolis Star-Tribune,* Peterson said about

Attendance at Saints games increased as Bush's entertaining, and sometimes controversial, game play drew the attention of football fans. His life off the field also became more colorful as he acquired endorsement deals and began dating reality television star Kim Kardashian.

Bush, "He's blessed. He's definitely gifted. I respect his game, respect his style as a running back and I cheer for him. I look forward for him to do good."

OPENING THE 2007 SEASON

Bush stayed in Los Angeles during the 2007 off-season, training on his own, before returning to New Orleans for preseason camp. The Saints had a mediocre 3–2 record in the preseason, and the regular season did not go particularly well either.

In the first regular-season game, the defending Super Bowl champs, the Indianapolis Colts, stomped the Saints 41–10. The next game was also a loss, with the Saints falling 31–14 to the Tampa Bay Buccaneers. Bush did not have outstanding numbers in either game. For example, in week two's contest, he rushed for only 27 yards, over a third of which came on one play, for an average of 2.7 yards per carry.

The Saints lost their next two games, too. In week three, they lost 31–14 to the Tennessee Titans. One of the game's high points, however, was Bush's first touchdown of the season, from the one-yard line. It was the first of two he scored that day. The team had a bye during week four, and week five against the Carolina Panthers resulted in a humiliating 16–13 defeat that was notable, at least in part, for Bush's career high of 21 carries.

During this period, Bush's role in the Saints lineup underwent a dramatic change. His fellow tailback, Deuce McAllister, had been battling knee problems since 2005. That season, McAllister was placed on the injured reserve list after tearing the anterior cruciate ligament (ACL) in his right knee, returning to the lineup in 2006. As the 2007 season began, McAllister appeared to be in good enough shape to be a starter again.

Then, in the week three home game against the Titans, McAllister was badly hurt: He again tore an anterior cruciate ligament, this time in his left knee. McAllister was out for the season, and it was time for Bush to step in as the team's starting tailback.

Bush's first game in this role came against Carolina on October 7. This game marked the first time since high school that Bush was a featured tailback. At USC, Bush and LenDale White had always shared the load. Then, as a pro, Bush and McAllister had worked together before McAllister's injury.

Some observers were skeptical about the change in the lineup. In large part, this doubt concerned Bush's relatively small size. Many fans and commentators questioned whether he could handle the extra pressure, both physical and emotional, of being an every-down back.

Bush dismissed the criticism, however. He noted that a number of outstanding running backs, including Barry Sanders, Warrick Dunn, Marshall Faulk, and Tiki Barber, were relatively small. As Bush pointed out, these athletes had done just fine despite their size.

In any case, Bush was excited and primed for his new role. He said that he definitely felt he had the attributes needed to be a successful every-down back. These included, in his opinion, longevity as well as the ability to quickly judge when to go down, when to get out of bounds, and when to seize an opportunity. For his part, Coach Sean Payton stated many times that he had full confidence in his starting back.

In the second week with Bush as featured back, the Saints began a four-game winning streak. Unfortunately, injuries continued to hamper the team in the second half of the season, including damage to Bush. In game nine, on November 4 against the Jacksonville Jaguars, Bush suffered his own knee problems. He partially tore the posterior cruciate ligament in his left knee. (On the bright side, the Saints soundly beat Jacksonville, 41–24.)

"HE'S A TOUGHER KID THAN PEOPLE REALIZE"

Bush sat out a couple of practices but was able to continue to play for a month before aggravating the injury in another game. He was forced to quit playing for the season. Fortunately, doctors determined that Bush did not require surgery, just physical rehabilitation and rest.

Nonetheless, the back missed the last four games of the regular season. A spokesman for the league told ESPN, "It just got to the point … where he couldn't [play] anymore. He's a

An injury to Saints player Deuce McAllister thrust Bush into the role of featured tailback for the team. Bush proved to be an effective tailback but was injured in a game against the Jacksonville Jaguars.

tougher kid than people realize, but it was only getting worse. At this point, he's just really beaten up."

Meanwhile, the Saints were limping along. After their unexpectedly promising play-off run in 2006, powered by McAllister and Bush, 2007 was a serious disappointment. The Saints stumbled to a 7–9 record for the year.

As for Bush, his numbers for the season were only decent, not spectacular. He had 6 touchdowns, 581 yards rushing and 417 yards receiving in 12 games. His longest run was 22 yards and his longest reception was 25.

In part, of course, Bush's mediocre record could be chalked up to the games he missed. Based on his performance in the first part of the season, however, many observers began to question how good Bush really was. As the excitement over the arrival of "Saint Reggie" wore off, and as his disappointing second season came to a close, they began to wonder: Could Bush fulfill his earlier promise?

It was a serious question. During his dazzling rookie year, Bush had drawn glowing comparisons to the greatest running backs of the game, including the legendary Hall of Famer Gale Sayers. Even before being hurt, however, Bush had fought to prove himself up to the hype. For him, the season that just ended had had as many lowlights as highlights. Fans were not happy, to say the least, and he sometimes had to endure insulting crowd chants of "B-U-S-T" when he took the field.

Bush was also criticized beyond his mediocre 2007 performance. Previously, the athlete had spent the off-season at his home in Los Angeles, not in New Orleans with his teammates. He had also been preoccupied with distractions such as endorsement deals, celebrity appearances, and his romance with Kardashian. Many players and observers saw his attitude as standoffish, demonstrating a reluctance to be a team player.

"I SEE A GUY WHO'S HUNGRY"

When he worked out on his own during the 2007 off-season, Bush had taken up a training regimen called *fre flo do*. He worked with the trainer who developed this discipline three or four times a week, for at least 90 minutes per session. Fre flo do combines Asian-inspired workouts with high-tech machines. Its inventor says that it approximates the frenetic nature of football, where split-second decisions have to be made under great pressure and an athlete must react quickly to avoid injury.

To improve his performance and public perception, Bush changed his ways as the 2008 season ramped up. He moved full time to New Orleans, attended the Saints' grueling workouts, and in general refocused himself on the game and his relationships with his teammates. In the Martel article, Bush said:

> I know I'm not a bust. I know I'm far from it. I know there's a lot of hard work, focus, patience, and determination. It'll all come to pass. You've just got to weather the storm while it's there and just continue to work your way through it.

Several teammates expressed their confidence in Bush as the new season drew closer. Now, his teammates noted, he genuinely seemed to have a renewed commitment to the team and a sharper focus on the game.

One of these players was Jon Stinchcomb. Quoted in a *Sports Illustrated* article by Damon Hack, the tackle said, "I see a guy who's hungry." In an interview with the Associated Press, Drew Brees elaborated on this opinion:

> He definitely made a point to be here, and I think that was important just for team camaraderie and so guys can actually see how hard he's working and know he's paying the price. I've definitely seen the change in

Reggie, just the level of focus, and I think a calmness, knowing he's put himself in the best position right now to be the type of player he wants to be.

"NASA MAY HAVE TO GET INVOLVED"

The Saints kicked off the 2008 season on a strong note, beating the Buccaneers 24–20. It appeared that Bush's newly recharged commitment was going to pay off. The back ran 14 times for 51 yards, and made a thrilling third-down 42-yard catch-and-run out of the backfield for a diving touchdown. He juked

"THE BEST CHANCE TO WIN"

In November of the 2007 season, Saints general manager Mickey Loomis spoke to a reporter about doubts that some people had over Reggie Bush's prospects. In an article by Jim Trotter *in Sports Illustrated*, Loomis said:

> We're not in any way displeased with Reggie's production. In fact we're very pleased. Just because it's not in a traditional running back sense doesn't mean a thing. The end goal is to win games and to be a good offense. I know this, we were the No. 1 offense last year with Reggie Bush as one of our featured weapons. I think that speaks for itself.
>
> Reggie draws a lot of attention from opposing defenses, so even when he doesn't get the ball he's affecting the play. One thing that's great about Reggie is that he wants to do as much as he can, but at the same time he wants to win. I've never seen him express any dissatisfaction with what he's being asked to do, because he realizes that the way we're doing things gives us the best chance to win.

Tampa Bay safety Jermaine Phillips at the 25-yard line and stiff-armed cornerback Phillip Buchanon at the 5 before diving for the goal line.

The touchdown was even sweeter because Phillips had been taunting Bush one play earlier. In an Associated Press article recapping the game, Bush said, "The play before he was talking trash, and the next play he was on my highlight tape."

During the game, Bush had ample chances to display his characteristic skill in playing in space. *USA Today* writer Larry Weisman noted, "That's where his talents lie and where he made the signature play of the [game]. . . . The New Orleans Saints talk so often about getting Reggie Bush 'in space' that eventually NASA may have to get involved."

MOVING FAST

Bush's performance continued to improve as the season progressed. For instance, in week three's game—a narrow loss to the Denver Broncos, 34–32—he had 18 carries for 73 yards, 11 receptions for 75 yards, and two touchdowns. The first of these was a smooth run up the middle, then to the outside, for 23 yards. His second touchdown came on a six-yard swing pass from Brees near the goal line.

Another notable game for Bush came on October 6, in a home matchup against the Minnesota Vikings. This time, he returned two punts for touchdowns and nearly had a third. This feat tied the league record for single-game punt returns for touchdowns; Bush was only the twelfth player ever to achieve the record. Unfortunately, the back-and-forth game was not as satisfying for the Saints. After making a number of blunders, the team lost 30–27 in a victory for the Vikings.

FASTER THAN FAST

During the game, Bush took part in a dramatic experiment. For the first time in public, ESPN used new optical-tracking technology to measure the speed of a football player. The company hopes that this technology may someday provide a standard statistic for the game, just as the speed of baseball pitches is routinely measured.

In the game, the optical-tracking technology was set up to measure either Bush or his Vikings counterpart Adrian Peterson, whoever got a long play first. As it turned out, that was Bush.

The experiment revealed that Bush reached a top speed of 22 miles per hour (35 kilometers per hour) on one of his two punt returns for touchdowns. This staggered observers—Bush's speed was startlingly close to the average speed that Jamaican sprinter Usain Bolt had achieved in the 100-meter dash at the 2008 Beijing Olympics. During that event, Bolt achieved an average speed of 23.07 miles per hour—fast enough to set a new world record of 9.69 seconds.

Bush's measured speed also put him ahead of the top speeds of several other elite sprinters. Among these were Maurice Greene (21.0 mph, or 33.8 kph, in the indoor 60 meters), Michael Johnson (20.71 mph, or 33.3 kph, in the 400 meters), and Florence Griffith-Joyner (21.32 mph, or 34.3 kph, in the 100).

Granted, these speeds were averages over the distances the athletes ran, as opposed to Bush's top speed at a single point. On the other hand, Bush was performing with significant handicaps. Journalist Sam Farmer, in an article published in the *Los Angeles Times*, pointed out, "[T]hose runners also weren't carrying a football and saddled with a helmet and pads."

A week later, at home battling the Raiders, Bush scored two more touchdowns (one on a 3-yard run and the other with a 15-yard reception). Bush did most of the work on the receiving score, evading Raider safety Gibril Wilson after a short catch over the middle. Nonetheless, Bush gave due credit to his teammates after the game. In particular, he praised Drew Brees. In an interview with the Associated Press, the back commented, "Fortunately for me, Drew likes to check the ball down to the running backs. It helps when you have a guy like that who can see the field and see the open guy."

During the game, Bush tied yet another NFL record, matching Arizona wide receiver Anquan Boldin for the shortest time needed to reach 200 catches. It took Bush only 34 games to get to this milestone. Furthermore, the team's performance against Oakland that day resulted in a dramatic and decisive win, 34–3.

INJURED AGAIN

The Saints had hoped to improve on their 7–9 record from the previous year. They did succeed in keeping a slim play-off hope alive for much of the season, but in the end they performed only slightly better than in 2007, finishing a mediocre 8–8.

Meanwhile, injury frustrated Bush's resurgence. On October 19, during a game against the Panthers, he injured his left knee again. He had surgery the next day to repair a torn meniscus and was forced to sit out four games.

Bush returned to action on November 30, in a contest against Tampa Bay, but his injury kept him from playing at full power. Then, on December 11, facing the Bears, Bush reinjured the knee.

The damage was diagnosed as a medial collateral ligament sprain, not a more serious tear. Still, the Saints had to determine what they were going to do with Bush. Besides the fact that Bush had undergone surgery on the same knee earlier, other factors played into New Orleans's decision. For one thing, the Saints were by now out of the play-off picture. Furthermore, only two games were left in the season.

So the Saints decided to put Bush on the injured reserve list again, ending his season early for the second year in a row. In an article in the *Baton Rouge Advocate*, Sean Payton commented:

> It's an MCL sprain, and for him right now, it's going to be rehab and rest. We feel pretty optimistic about what he has. He wouldn't have been put on IR if we had more

Bush's success on the field is credited to his remarkable speed. In a 2008 game against the Minnesota Vikings, Bush tied the league record for single game punt returns for touchdowns and was clocked at an impressive 22 miles (35.4 km) per hour.

than two or three weeks left in the season. In other words, the news is fairly good—which is encouraging.

WHAT WAS LACKING?

Bush finished the year with 106 carries for 404 rushing yards, 52 receptions for 440 yards, and nine touchdowns in 10 games. His statistics were not bad but not good enough to satisfy him. In Bush's opinion, he had been performing below expectations even before his injury. He had worked hard but had still fallen short.

Not everyone felt the same way. Some observers thought that he was not appreciated enough. One such commentator was *Sports Illustrated* journalist Peter King, who stated that Bush's accomplishments as a constant scoring threat were being overlooked.

In his column, which was written before Bush was injured, King noted that Bush's number of touchdowns was the most so far that season. He also wrote that it was unrealistic to expect Bush to turn every touch into a game-changing play. King noted, "To call him a bust . . . is misguided and wrong. He's an effective situational back and an explosive return man, a player who should give New Orleans 12 to 14 touchdowns a year (he has 23 in 34 career games) as long as he stays healthy."

A number of fans agreed with King. On the other hand, many—perhaps most—observers felt that, in Bush's first three seasons as a pro, he had failed to live up to the hype surrounding him.

They agreed that during those years he had been nothing more than a very good player who could display moments of brilliance on the field. Journalist Sam Farmer summed up these sentiments in an October 2008 article:

> He made some big plays [early in his pro career], yet also disappeared for long stretches. He didn't score a touchdown, rushing or receiving, until the ninth game

of his rookie season. Long gone were his get-it-and-split-it days of USC, when he'd get a handoff and knife untouched right through the middle of a defense.... [However], this season, the Saints are starting to really cash in on Bush's remarkable ability to run and catch.

So Bush ended the year with a mixed assessment. Despite this inconsistent report and despite his injuries, the running back looked forward to the future.

The Big Game and the Next Steps

Of course, no one knows exactly what the future will hold for Bush's career and private life. Many observers—and Bush himself—have high expectations. On the other hand, many others have serious reservations about what might happen.

RETURNING FROM THE INJURED LIST

One question has been the status of his health. In the spring of 2009, Bush had further surgery on his troubled left knee. He then faced months of intensive physical therapy.

He was able to attend the Saints training camp prior to the 2009 season, although with an iced knee as a safeguard. Bush also sat out some of the practices. In an Associated Press article, the athlete said, "I iced it just as a precaution, so when I ice it, that means I'm just maintaining. I've got to stay on top of it and treat it as if it was the first day I injured it."

Coach Sean Payton echoed Bush's confidence. In an article by Gary Mihoces in *USA Today,* the coach said during camp:

> No, I feel pretty good about his health right now. I feel real good about the camp he's having. I want to continue to feel that way. I'm encouraged about where he's at right now. He's fine. You watch him out here at practice when he's out there and you watch him run. I feel positive about it, but just want to monitor it.

CONTROVERSY

Another serious issue that Bush had to deal with in recent years concerned allegations that he was guilty of improper behavior while at USC. Specifically, the accusations charged that Bush and his family accepted substantial cash and gifts during his last year there. These actions clearly violated NCAA rules.

The accusations against Bush were first made in April 2006, just a week before the NFL Draft. The controversy exploded in the media, fizzled out for some time, and then resurfaced.

The people who made the allegations against Bush were two would-be sports agents, Michael Michaels and Lloyd Lake. While Bush was still at USC, they had formed New Era, an agency that would have had Bush as its main client. After Bush turned pro, however, he decided to sign with Mike Ornstein, another sports marketing agent, and New Era folded.

Ornstein aggressively worked to sign his newly famous client to many profitable endorsements, which would soon make the athlete millions of dollars. There were problems, however. According to Michaels and Lake, Ornstein persuaded Bush to sign with him by offering improper benefits, mostly in cash. Specifically, the two produced what they said was documented evidence that Bush and his family received about $280,000 in illegal payments. They also accused Bush of failing to pay for a new car and for a $3,000-a-month condominium while at USC.

Furthermore, they alleged that Bush's family lived for a time in an expensive house in Spring Valley, California, during the athlete's last year in college, but never paid rent. This would also be an improper gift under NCAA rules.

INVESTIGATIONS

A series of investigative articles published by Yahoo! Sports partially backed up these accusations. The reports claimed to have found documented evidence of rules violations, including hotel and credit card receipts and audiotapes.

Concerned about maintaining his client's public image, Ornstein urged Bush to end the controversy by settling the case out of court—that is, for a cash settlement before a jury trial took place. Members of Bush's family, however, apparently did not agree.

Bush ended up settling only with Michaels, who had remained relatively quiet during the controversy. The amount Michaels received was not revealed, but is estimated to be about $200,000.

Meanwhile, Lake was very public about his accusations against Bush. He filed a lawsuit against the athlete, seeking about $300,000 that he claims to have spent on New Era. Lake even contributed to a book, *Tarnished Heisman*, detailing his side of the story.

Unlike Michaels, a successful businessman, Lake is a convicted felon with documented gang attachments. A jury might therefore consider his testimony unreliable. Bush's attorney, David Cornwell, repeatedly dismissed Lake's claims as untrue. He characterized the lawsuit as a form of extortion.

"IT'S NOT STEROIDS, NOT DOG-FIGHTING, NOT MURDER"

Then, in 2007, Bush fired Ornstein. The reasons for the split were never made public. The speculation in the media, however, was that the firing resulted from disagreements over the handling of the controversy—specifically, Ornstein's opinion that the family should have settled out of court.

Many observers have harshly criticized the two would-be sports agents, as well as Ornstein. On the other hand, not everyone who has followed the controversy considers it too serious. In their eyes, accepting gifts is a minor offense compared with the crimes some other professional athletes have committed.

One of these observers is Bob Dorfman, a San Francisco advertising executive and the author of the semiannual *Sports Marketers' Scouting Report*. In a *Los Angeles Times* article, Dorfman commented, "It's not steroids, not dog-fighting, not murder.... I think a lot of fans will say, 'Ah, it's just another case of them coming down on somebody for something that's arbitrary.'"

THE RESULTS OF THE INVESTIGATION

In April 2009, the NCAA announced that it was combining the investigation with that of another former USC athlete, basketball player O.J. Mayo. Mayo had also been accused of accepting illegal gifts, in this case from a middleman representing a sports agency. In June 2009, Trojans basketball coach Tim Floyd resigned because of the investigation. He had also been accused of providing money to the middleman.

The combined Bush-Mayo inquiry became a probe into the school's entire athletic program. USC athletic director Mike Garrett stated that his department was cooperating fully to protect its reputation. He told a reporter for the *Los Angeles Times*, "People who say that we have something to protect are partially right. What we have to protect is the integrity of the athletic department. And that means doing this right. And that is what we are doing."

For his part, Bush remained calm and unworried about the accusations, at least publicly. He maintained that he was not guilty and said that he would not let the situation distract him from his game. In an article on the Saints' Web site, Bush said:

> It hasn't been a distraction. I've been so focused on this [2009] season and what I can control. We had a great

run this year. I can't control everything else that goes on with USC and with what's going on there. Obviously, I'm four years removed from college now. SC is still in my heart, and always will be. I'll be the first one to do anything I can to show my support to USC.

In time, the investigation did find USC guilty of violations, with consequences that were serious for both Bush and the university. The USC football program was barred from bowl games in 2010 and 2011 and lost 30 scholarships over three years. Bush was stripped of his eligibility, beginning in December 2004 and including the entire 2005 season, which negated many of his college-era awards and records. As a result, Bush voluntarily gave back his Heisman Trophy in September 2010. In addition, Bush settled the lawsuit brought by Lake out of court in April 2010.

PERSONAL LIFE

Of course, while dealing with the scandal and maintaining his football career, Bush has also had an active private life. Despite his dislike of media attention, this part of his world is being partially lived in the spotlight. Perhaps the most significant turn of events in this area was his temporary breakup with Kim Kardashian in the summer of 2008.

Publicly, the couple said that they broke up because their schedules were increasingly busy and they were forced to spend too much time away from each other. For at least half of the year, Bush was in New Orleans and Kardashian in Los Angeles. According to an unnamed source quoted in *People* magazine at the time, "They never get to see each other, ever. It's been a long time coming. They still love each other and are part of [each other's] lives, but . . . it's tough."

The split, however, was short-lived, and the two were soon back together. In fact, rumors flew that they were engaged. Asked by a Fox News reporter if she would relocate to New Orleans if they married, Kardashian replied, "Of course. I am

REGGIE BUSH

REGGIE BUSH - 2005

FIFTH IN THE 2004 VOTING, REGGIE BUSH BECAME USC'S FIRST TAILBACK SINCE 1981 TO WIN THE HEISMAN WHEN HE DID SO IN 2005 WITH THE HIGHEST PERCENTAGE OF POINTS EVER. HE HAD 6,817 CAREER ALL-PURPOSE YARDS, (WITH 99 PLAYS OF 20-PLUS YARDS), AND LED THE NATION IN 2005 WITH A PAC-10 RECORD 2,890 YARDS, INCLUDING A LEAGUE RECORD 513 AGAINST FRESNO STATE. HE AVERAGED A PAC-10 RECORD 8.7 YARDS PER RUSH IN 2005.

When an NCAA investigation concluded that Bush and his family inappropriately accepted gifts during his time at USC, the organization punished Bush and the university. Bush was stripped of his athletic achievements, and his jersey display was removed from the school's Heritage Hall (*above*). In addition, he voluntarily returned his Heisman Trophy.

there all the time anyway. . . . [I]t takes a lot to be in a long distance relationship especially when the both of us have so much going on. It is an adjustment to say OK, we have to make this [a] priority and we've done that and it is better than ever." They eventually broke up for good.

Another aspect of Bush's life that will no doubt continue is his interest in clothes and fashion. It is still important for him to look good. Needless to say, the running back's teammates tease him about it—especially about how long it takes for him to get ready. Reporter Brent Schrotenboer wrote that the athlete's closet "might be the only place Bush stays still for more than a few minutes."

Bush defends his habit by saying, "I don't just like to throw on clothes and mismatches and whatever. I like to look presentable. I sometimes do take a little longer to get dressed than a woman."

REGGIE HONORS HIS ROOTS

One aspect of Bush's personal life that is also part of his professional life concerns a game-time habit. Ever since his days at USC, the athlete has written a slogan on the black antiglare tape under his eyes. He adds either "619" (San Diego's area code) or "S.E." (for Southeast San Diego). This is his way of honoring his hometown roots. In an interview with journalist Schrotenboer, Bush's stepfather, LaMar Griffin, said, "Reggie remembers when we didn't have a lot of money, and we had to make do with what we had. He didn't have a lot of clothes."

Of course, Bush has come a long way from those modest beginnings. Besides his multimillion-dollar salary, he has made millions landing commercial endorsements. For example, among the endorsement contracts Bush has recently signed is one with Red Bull energy drink.

Also big earners for him are various items of memorabilia. And his jersey has been one of the NFL's most popular ever since his rookie year. As he did early in his pro career, Bush has continued to donate much of this income to charities.

"THE GUY BACK THERE"

Bush's playing career entered a new phase early in 2009, when the Saints released Deuce McAllister, the franchise's all-time leading rusher (with 6,069 yards). The Saints let McAllister go so the team could get under the salary cap.

In an article in the Houma, Louisiana, *Courier*, Bush said that he thought the Saints were looking to him to be their key player. This was true, he said, even though fellow running back Pierre Thomas led the Saints in 2008 with 625 yards and nine touchdowns, compared to Bush's 404 yards and two rushing touchdowns.

Bush nonetheless remained confident and positive. He said, "They're looking for me to be the guy back there.... By the moves that they're making, it definitely speaks volumes to me as to what I need to prepare myself for."

Not everyone was as optimistic about Bush's chances for an outstanding 2009 season. For example, in an August column for SI.com, commentator Phil Taylor wrote that Bush had never been able to live up to the hype that surrounded him in his college years and his first year with the Saints. Admitting that he had to revise his earlier glowing comments about Bush, Taylor wrote:

> At this point in his career, he's more well-known for having dated reality show hottie Kim Kardashian than for anything he's done for the Saints on the field. If Bush doesn't get it in gear, he's in danger of falling into the same category as Kardashian—celebrities who are famous even though we can't quite remember why....
>
> He would be wise to lay off the starlets, the Hollywood scene and the endorsements for a while and make sure

Fellow Saints player Deuce McAllister worked with Bush to present a strong pair of tailbacks for the team. When McAllister was released from the team in 2009, Bush became the Saints' big star.

all of his mental and physical energy is devoted to football. There is still the possibility, although it's growing slimmer, that Bush could eventually live up to his billing as a great back.

A MAGICAL SEASON

As it turned out, the 2009 season was a magical one for the Saints, who proved that they had come a long way from the days when they were the Aints. It was, far and away, the best season the franchise has had, and the year ended with a spectacular bang.

The Saints won the first 13 games of the season, setting a record for the longest undefeated season opening by an National Football Conference team since the AFL–NFL merger (the previous record was held by the 1985 Chicago Bears). Bush was a contributor to the team's strength, rushing for 390 yards (with a 5.6 yards-per-carry average), catching 47 passes for 335 yards, and adding another 130 yards returning punts for the season.

After this remarkable run, the Saints lost their last three games, falling to the Dallas Cowboys, Tampa Bay Buccaneers, and Carolina Panthers to finish the season at 13–3. Still, the Saints were the top seed in the NFC—for the first time ever—and had a bye in the first round of the play-offs.

The Saints' postseason began when they faced the Arizona Cardinals, the defending NFC champions. Arizona was looking strong, fresh off a 51–45 overtime win over the Green Bay Packers, during which the Cardinals racked up 531 yards against a defense that was ranked second in the league in total yards allowed.

New Orleans, however, proved to be stronger. Arizona scored on the first play of the game, but after that it was downhill for the defending champs. The Saints cruised to 35 points in the first half (as opposed to the Cardinals' 14) and continued to dominate. Bush contributed to this push with 217 all-purpose yards, including an 83-yard punt return and a franchise play-off record 46-yard touchdown run. At the end of the day, it was a decisive victory: 45–14.

HEADED TO THE SUPER BOWL

Next up was the NFC Championship Game, which the Superdome was hosting for the first time. This game pitted the Saints against the Minnesota Vikings on January 24, 2010. The Vikings were led by an 11-time Pro Bowl quarterback, the legendary Brett Favre. The quarterback was a formidable opponent, having thrown four touchdown passes during the Vikings' divisional round play-off win over the Dallas Cowboys the week before.

The Saints' offense could garner only 257 total yards during the game. Bush gained only eight yards rushing on seven carries and two receptions for 33 yards. His performance, many observers pointed out, displayed both his worst and best characteristics as a player.

Bush fumbled a punt, for instance, and turned the ball over near the Saints' goal line. On the other hand, the back excelled when Brees, under pressure, rolled out of the pocket. Bush sensed the flow, ran an ad-lib pass route, got open, caught the toss from Brees, fought off a tackle, and dove into the front corner of the end zone with the ball extended, for a touchdown that proved vital to the Saints' game.

Despite the overall disappointing performance by the Saints' offense, the defense made up for the downturn by forcing five turnovers. The contest's decisive play came in the fourth quarter, with the score tied 28–28 and the Vikings driving for a potential game-winning field goal. With less than a minute left, Minnesota reached the Saints' 33-yard line. After two runs for no gain and a penalty, the Vikings were pushed back to the 38. On the next play, Saints cornerback Tracy Porter stopped what looked like Minnesota's game-winning drive by picking off a pass by Favre.

The interception sent the game into overtime—and, naturally, it also sent the hometown crowd in the Superdome skyrocketing into a frenzy. New Orleans won the coin toss, and Pierre Thomas's 40-yard kickoff return set up a 10-play, 39-yard drive that ended with a game-winning 40-yard field goal by Garrett Hartley.

The contest was over, 31–28. The crowd went nuts, and the Saints were headed to their first-ever Super Bowl to face the Indianapolis Colts.

WHO DAT?

Immediately after the Saints' stunning victory, delirious fans from all across New Orleans, including thousands streaming out of the Superdome, spontaneously started chanting while parading down the city's famed Bourbon Street: "Who dat, who dat, who dat in the Super Bowl?"

The phrase was a variation on a familiar one. Versions of the chant "Who dat? Who dat? Who dat say dey gonna beat dem Saints?" go back decades. The chant has appeared elsewhere in sports, but it has been an integral part of the world of Saints fans since the franchise's beginnings. In fact, use of the phrase has become so widespread that New Orleans fans are known as the Who Dat Nation.

Residents of New Orleans were by no means the only ones rooting for the Saints. People across the nation—even those who were not necessarily sports fans—got caught up in the excitement.

Even President Barack Obama, famously a basketball fan, remarked that he would closely watch the game. He told the Associated Press, "I guess I am rooting a little bit for the Saints as the underdog, partly just because . . . I think about what's happened in New Orleans over the last several years and how much that team means to them. You know, I'm pretty sympathetic."

Meanwhile, as the Who Dat Nation and the team prepared for the biggest of all games, Bush told reporters that, remarkably, he felt calm. He said he was not fazed by the hoopla over the Saints' contest with the Indianapolis Colts, or by the feeling that he was not playing up to his potential after recovering from microfracture surgery on his injured knee. In a *New York Times* article by Joe Lapointe, Bush said, "I've always envisioned myself playing in big games. It feels like home. It feels like this is where I'm supposed to be. I don't feel overwhelmed. There is a sense of calmness."

IT'S A HUGE GAME

On the other hand, Bush freely admitted to being excited about the big game in Miami. Quoted on the Saints' Web site, he said:

> It's a huge game. I don't want to say it's the biggest game of my life, but it is. It's the biggest game of my career at this point. When I think about all the great players, guys who haven't yet, but will get a chance to play in

the Super Bowl, I feel blessed. To be able to be here right now is a blessing. To be able to have experienced a championship game at every level—high school, college, and now the Super Bowl—it's a blessing.

It could be another 10, 15 years, or I could never be back in the Super Bowl. You never know when your next chance will be ... and I'm just trying to take it all in right now. Enjoy it, remember these times, but at the same time remember that we still have a football game to win.

Besides feeling confident about his own playing strength, Bush also had faith in his team. He pointed out that, a few years earlier, in 2007, when the Colts won their first Super Bowl after moving from Baltimore, they had relatively little experience in big games. Now it was the Saints' turn. In an article on the Saints' Web site, the running back commented, "Experience helps a lot [but we] can't really worry about the experience level. Obviously, that would help us if we had been there before, but we haven't. This is our first time." He added with understatement, "You know, it's tough to get here."

Bush clearly felt that the Saints' running game would be crucial to success. Time and again throughout his career, he had expressed his opinion that the running back sets the tone for the game. On the Saints' Web site, he remarked, "We can't allow the Indianapolis Colts to slow down our running attack, because we need a balanced attack to win this game. If you look back, the teams who have won the Super Bowl, they ran the ball well.... We have to run the ball well if we want to even have a fighting chance to win this game."

VICTORY!

The big day finally arrived: Super Bowl XLIV was held on February 7, 2010, at Sun Life Stadium in Miami Gardens, Florida. More than 106 million people tuned in—a new record for a televised program. The previous record, for the finale of the series *M*A*S*H*, had stood for more than a quarter-century.

Everyone in the Saints organization was as pumped as possible, and Bush was no exception. He told *New York Times* reporter Joe Lapointe that Coach Sean Payton had warned the running back that he would be used a lot. Bush said, "He told me just to be ready because my tongue was going to be hanging out. You have to love to hear your coach tell you, 'Hey, be ready for a big day.'"

WHO NEEDS THE VICTORY MORE?

During a press conference before the Super Bowl, reporters asked Reggie Bush which he thought needed a victory more: the team or the city of New Orleans. As stated on the Saints' Web site, the running back replied:

I think it's for everybody, but probably more so the city of New Orleans. This game is obviously huge for them. Being able to be a part of this run right now—the first New Orleans Saints team to make the Super Bowl—is special. We're excited to be here, but we still have a game to play. . . .

I think if we're able to bring a Super Bowl trophy to the city of New Orleans, it would be huge. It might be the single greatest event to ever happen in New Orleans. It would be more than just about football, just as the reopening of the Superdome was more than that game, that day. It was about Hurricane Katrina, the thousands of lives that were lost during that storm. The same thing applies, I think, to this game. We're going to try to do the best we can to bring it back home to New Orleans and give the city something to be proud about.

The Big Game and the Next Steps

The Colts started off strong, including a 96-yard scoring drive that tied the record for the longest drive in Super Bowl history. The first quarter ended with Indianapolis ahead, 10–0. The Saints whittled that lead down to 10–6 by the end of the first half, with Garrett Hartley kicking a pair of field goals.

At the start of the second half, the Saints surprised their opponents with an onside kick—a play the Saints coaches called "the Ambush." Thomas Morstead kicked the ball to his left, and it bounced off Colts wide receiver Hank Baskett, who was unable to make a clean recovery. A pileup developed over the loose ball, and the officials needed more than a minute to separate the players. Saints linebacker Jonathan Casillas was officially credited with recovery the ball, although he and other Saints players later said that it was actually safety Chris Reis.

The Saints' offense marched down the field on a 58-yard drive, during which they never faced a third down. Quarterback Drew Brees completed five consecutive passes and a screen pass to Pierre Thomas, who took the ball 16 yards to the end zone to give the Saints a 13–10 lead.

The Colts retaliated with a touchdown drive of their own, moving the ball 76 yards in 10 plays to put them back on top 17–13. Another field goal by Hartley brought the Saints to within one point of tying the game at the end of the quarter.

The fourth quarter featured another Brees-led touchdown drive with seven different players getting the ball, the first being Bush with a 12-yard run and the last being a touchdown pass to tight end Jeremy Shockey. The Saints went for a two-point conversion; wide receiver Lance Moore secured a pass and tried to stretch the ball over the goal line. He fell to the ground and rolled over on his head, and the ball came out of his hands. The play was ruled incomplete, but a challenge from Coach Payton overturned the ruling; Moore had maintained possession of the ball long enough, and the ball had crossed the plane of the goal line for a successful two-point conversion.

The Saints now had a 24–17 advantage. Peyton Manning led the Colts on a drive into Saints territory, but Tracy Porter intercepted a pass at the Saints' 26-yard line and returned it 74 yards for a touchdown. With a successful extra point, the Saints led 31–17 with 3:12 remaining.

Now down by two possessions, the Colts were able to drive to the Saints' 3-yard line. Although an offensive pass interference penalty on first and goal pushed them back 10 yards, the Colts retrieved those yards on the next play. Then the next three plays sealed the Colts' fate: a tipped pass that went off the goal post to fall incomplete, a loss of two yards on a rushing play, and an incomplete pass that went through the hands of wide receiver Reggie Wayne.

And that was it. The Saints had their first Super Bowl win in franchise history.

NEW ORLEANS IS A PARTY TOWN!

Everyone knew that New Orleans would go crazy if the Saints won. Before the contest, Super Bowl mania had seized the city. Mardi Gras parades, church services, and even jury trials had been rescheduled to make sure no one had to miss the kickoff.

Just before the game, Mayor Ray Nagin had confidently predicted a win. Remarking that New Orleans native Manning would have to take "a whipping on this one," the mayor told Marc Caputo, a reporter for the *Miami Herald*, "We don't riot. But we're going to party.... This town is going to have one heck of a celebration.... We're going to have a good time."

Nagin's town, already famous for wild behavior and raucous entertainment like Mardi Gras, did not disappoint him. Even the strippers on Bourbon Street, the main street in New Orleans's famously wide-open French Quarter, stopped dancing long enough to celebrate.

There were fireworks, strangers hugging, flags waving, cowbells shaking, car horns honking, brass bands playing, and dancing in the streets. Not to mention endless cries of "Who dat!" The headline in the next day's *Times-Picayune* newspaper summed it up in one word: "Amen!"

Two days after the game, the heroes of the moment were the guests of honor for a huge parade through the streets of downtown New Orleans. Saints players, coaches, and team owner Tom Benson rode carnival floats rolling past tens of thousands of cheering fans. They threw strings of beads into the crowd—a traditional Mardi Gras custom—and signed countless autographs. Coach Payton blew kisses and held the Lombardi Trophy, given to the winners of the Super Bowl, over his head as the city celebrated "Lombardi Gras."

THINKING ABOUT NEXT YEAR

Even before excitement over the victory began to die down, analysts and fans—as well as the Saints owners and coaches—started to think about the next season and the Super Bowl in Arlington, Texas. One of the most important questions was what would happen with Reggie Bush.

In his four seasons with the Saints, most analysts agreed, Bush had impressive flashes of brilliance. Sportswriter Glenn Guilbeau, writing in the Monroe, Louisiana, *News-Star*, commented, "He was not a factor in most of the Saints wins last season, but when he is used he can be deadly. He's like a Corvette in the garage. It's a luxury, and you might not be able to afford it. But you hate to get rid of it. You don't drive it to work. That's what [Pierre] Thomas is for, but Bush is there for that key weekend or special event like the NFC title game."

On the other hand, in the Super Bowl—arguably the most important contest of his career—Bush had only a so-so game. He did not start, he racked up only 25 yards rushing and 38 receiving, he had four receptions, and he scored no touchdowns. Other performances, notably the nearly perfect game of Drew Brees, had carried the day.

The 2010 season proved to be less magical than the season that brought the Saints their Super Bowl triumph. New Orleans

On February 7, 2010, Super Bowl XLIV became the most-watched event in television history as more than 106 million people tuned in to watch the New Orleans Saints play the Indianapolis Colts. Although the Saints won the game, their first championship in the franchise's history, Bush's future remains unclear.

qualified for the play-offs as a wild-card team but fell in the first round to the Seattle Seahawks. The season was even less magical for Bush, as he played in only eight games, missing the others with a broken bone in his right leg.

Overall, despite flashes of brilliance, Bush has been a disappointment in the eyes of many observers. In large part because of his injuries, Bush had not fulfilled the hype that preceded his arrival in New Orleans. In five regular seasons, he had 524 rushing attempts for 2,090 yards and 17 touchdowns, and 294 receptions for 2,142 yards and 12 touchdowns. Even when healthy, some felt, Bush had often provided more style than substance in his game.

Meanwhile, Bush's salary with the Saints had jumped from $2.5 million in 2009 to $8 million in 2010. Many fans and other observers felt that he was being overpaid for what he was contributing to the team, and there was widespread speculation that the Saints might renegotiate his salary. There was even the possibility that, like many other NFL players with high salaries and modest statistics, he would be vulnerable to release. Meanwhile, the rumors continued to fly, including one that would have Bush joining his coach from his USC days, Pete Carroll, who became the coach of the Seattle Seahawks after that team's dismal 2009 season.

As of early 2011, the future for Bush was still uncertain. He felt pretty sure that he would not be brought back to the Saints with his $11.8 million salary for the upcoming season still in place. He told reporter Brett Martel, in an article for the *Canadian Press*, "Common sense would tell you probably not. We'll see what happens. We'll see what we can do and how we can make this thing work." Bush made it clear that he wanted to remain a Saint and was willing to renegotiate his salary.

Meanwhile, many reporters and fans wondered what the future might bring. A number of them noted that Bush's off-and-on spurts of greatness kept them on edge. Sportswriter Shaneika Dabney commented on web site the Huffington Post, "When he's hot, he's unstoppable. When he's not, you want to throw him off the Mississippi River Bridge."

No matter who proves to be right about the future of Reggie Bush's career, one thing is clear. His record has been spotty, but when it has been good, it has been extraordinary. Bush will always be considered one of the greats of the game.

STATISTICS

REGGIE BUSH
POSITION: Running back

FULL NAME: Reginald Alfred Bush II
BORN: March 2, 1985, San Diego, California
HEIGHT: 6'0"
HEIGHT: 203 lbs.
COLLEGE: University of Southern California
TEAM: New Orleans Saints (2006–)

YEAR	TEAM	G	ATT	YARDS	Y/C	TD	REC	YARDS	Y/R	TD
2006	NO	16	155	565	3.6	6	88	742	8.4	2
2007	NO	12	157	581	3.7	4	73	417	5.7	2
2008	NO	10	106	404	3.8	2	52	440	8.5	4
2009	NO	14	70	390	5.6	5	47	335	7.1	3
2010	NO	8	36	150	4.2	0	34	208	6.1	1
TOTALS		60	524	2,090	4.0	17	294	2,142	7.3	12

CHRONOLOGY

1985   Reginald Alfred Bush II is born on March 2, 1985, at Sharp Memorial Hospital in San Diego, California.

1994   Reggie joins the Grossmont/La Mesa Mighty Mite Warriors in the Pop Warner League. In his first official game, he rushes for 544 yards on 27 carries, kicks three extra points, scores eight touchdowns, catches one pass, makes two tackles, and recovers a fumble—all in a 32-minute game.

1999   Enters his freshman year at Helix High School in nearby La Mesa; in his first scrimmage as a freshman, completes a 60-yard run.

2000   Named to All-State team as a sophomore at Helix High.

2001   Helps lead Helix High to the state championship game; is again named to the All-State team.

2002   Named to *Parade* magazine's prestigious All-American list as a high school senior.

2003   Graduates from high school and begins his freshman year at the University of Southern California. The 1,331 total yards he racks up for the year are the most ever by a freshman in USC history.

2004   USC has another remarkable season, finishing 12–0 and winning the Orange Bowl (where they pummeled Oklahoma 55–19) to earn the national title. Bush is named the team's Most Valuable Player.

2005   Bush wins the Heisman Trophy, and USC has another great season, going to the Rose Bowl.

2006   Declares for the NFL Draft and is chosen with the number two pick overall by the New Orleans Saints. Signs a six-year contract that could earn him a potential $62 million. Is warmly welcomed by the football fans of New Orleans as symbol of renewed hope in the wake of Hurricane Katrina.

Allegations surface of improper actions taken by Bush, his family, and his agent during his USC career.

2007 The Saints advance to the NFC Championship Game in January but lose to the Chicago Bears. Bush begins an on-again, off-again relationship with reality-TV star Kim Kardashian.

Becomes part of the Saints' starting lineup after Deuce McAllister is injured. Injures his knee in game nine of the season. A month later, he is forced to sit out the rest of the season.

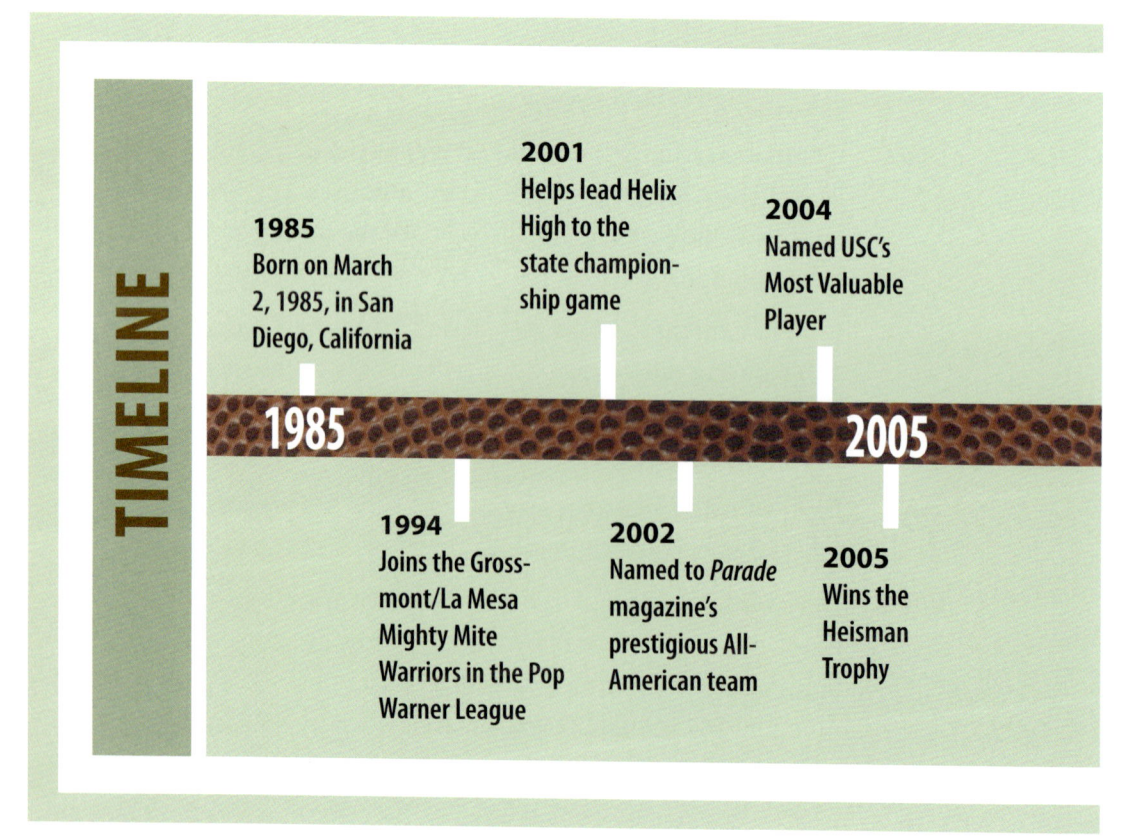

TIMELINE

1985 Born on March 2, 1985, in San Diego, California

2001 Helps lead Helix High to the state championship game

2004 Named USC's Most Valuable Player

1985 — **2005**

1994 Joins the Grossmont/La Mesa Mighty Mite Warriors in the Pop Warner League

2002 Named to *Parade* magazine's prestigious All-American team

2005 Wins the Heisman Trophy

Chronology

2008 Gets off to a strong start but is injured again in October and undergoes surgery. Returns to the lineup briefly but is forced to sit out the final two games.

2009 Undergoes additional surgery on one of his damaged knees and sits out some preseason practices.

NCAA combines the ongoing investigation of Bush's alleged improper activity at USC with that of former USC basketball star O.J. Mayo.

During the regular season, the Saints win their first 13 games and go on to be the NFC's top seed in the play-offs.

2010 The Saints win Super Bowl over the Indianapolis Colts, 31–17.

REGGIE BUSH

2007 Saints advance to the NFC Championship Game but lose to the Chicago Bears

2006 New Orleans Saints draft Bush with the number two pick overall

2010 Saints win Super Bowl over the Indianapolis Colts, 31–17

2010 NCAA issues sanctions against USC related to violations involving Bush; Bush voluntarily returns his Heisman Trophy

The NCAA issues sanctions against USC related to violations involving Bush. Bush's eligibility beginning in December 2004 and including the entire 2005 season is revoked. Bush voluntarily returns his Heisman Trophy.

GLOSSARY

American Football Conference (AFC)   One of the two conferences in the National Football League. The AFC was established after the NFL merged with the American Football League (AFL) in 1970.

bowl game   A game played by college football teams after the regular season. It is considered a reward for a successful season. Some of the more famous bowl games are the Rose Bowl, the Sugar Bowl, and the Fiesta Bowl.

carry   A run with the ball, also known as a rush or rushing attempt.

draft   The selection of collegiate players for entrance into the National Football League. Typically, the team with the worst record in the previous season picks first in the draft.

drive   A series of plays by the offensive team that begins when they get the ball and ends when they score or turn the ball over to the other team.

handoff   When a player gives the ball to a teammate behind or beside him, instead of passing it forward.

Heisman Trophy   An award presented annually to the most outstanding player in college football.

linebacker   A defensive player usually lined up behind the defensive linemen and in front of the defensive secondary.

line of scrimmage   A moving imaginary line that stretches across the width of the field to the sidelines and separates the two teams before the play begins.

National Football Conference (NFC)   One of two conferences in the National Football League. The NFC was established after the NFL merged with the American Football League (AFL) in 1970.

offensive lineman   An offensive player lined up very near the line of scrimmage, usually a center, guard, or tackle; his job is to block for runners and passers.

Glossary

offseason   The period between a team's final game and the beginning of preseason training camp.

onside kick   A play in which the kicking team tries to recover the ball by kicking it a short distance down the field.

pass   A throw from one player to another. A forward pass goes down the field, and a lateral pass (also just called a lateral) goes backward or parallel to the line of scrimmage.

play-offs   The postseason games up to and including the Super Bowl. A team must either win its division or have one of the two best records in the conference to make the play-offs.

preseason   The period of time before the regular season during which teams train, evaluate players, and play exhibition games.

quarterback   The player who directs the offense by calling or relaying the play and then receiving the snap and initiating a run or throw.

receiver   Offensive player who catches passes, usually either a wide receiver, tight end, or running back.

running back   An offensive player, also called a "back," whose main job is to run with the football and gain yards, block for other runners or the quarterback, or catch short passes. Halfbacks, fullbacks, and tailbacks are all backs with varying assignments, skills, and positions.

Super Bowl   The championship game of the NFL, pitting the champions of the AFC and the NFC against each other.

touchdown   A play worth six points in which any part of the ball while legally in the possession of a player crosses the plane of the opponent's goal line. A touchdown allows the team a chance for one extra point by kicking the ball or two points by running or passing the ball into the end zone.

two-point conversion   A scoring play, immediately after a touchdown, in which a team can add two points by running or passing the ball into the end zone, starting from the opponent's 2-yard line.

wild card A team that does not win a division title but has the next best record in the conference. In each conference, two wild-card teams make the play-offs.

BIBLIOGRAPHY

Adamson, Mike. "Reggie Bush." *Guardian* (U.K.), June 19, 2008.

Associated Press. "Bush Joins Saints for Afternoon Practice After Taking Care of His Knee." NFL.com, August 5, 2009. Available online. URL: http://www.nfl.com/trainingcamp/story?id=09000d5d811adba4&template=without-video-with-comments&confirm=true.

Brinkley, Douglas. "Saint Reggie's Passion." *Sports Illustrated*, August 28, 2006.

"Bush Says He's Now the Man." *Courier* (Houma, Louisiana), April 6, 2009.

Caputo, Marc. "New Orleans Mayor Predicts Saints Win Followed by Mega-Drinking." *Miami Herald*, February 5, 2010.

Curtis, Jake. "USC Playmaker Reggie Bush Shines on Every Stage; Rose Bowl Final Warm-Up for NFL?" *San Francisco Chronicle*, January 3, 2006.

Deitsch, Richard. "Q&A: Reggie Bush." *Sports Illustrated*, April 21, 2006.

Farmer, Sam. "Saints' Bush Finally Reverting to Hype." *Los Angeles Times*, October 19, 2008.

Fleeman, Michael. "Kim Kardashian and Reggie Bush Call It Quits." *People*, July 27, 2009.

Greenstein, Teddy. "Titanic Trojan: For NFL Teams, USC's Reggie Bush Is the Most Sought-After College Player in Years." *Chicago Tribune*, January 2, 2006.

Gregory, Sean. "Did You See That?" *Time*, December 19, 2005.

Guilbeau, Glenn. "New Orleans Is No One-Year Wonder." *News-Star* (Monroe, Louisiana), February 14, 2010.

Hack, Damon. "Reappearing Act." *Sports Illustrated*, September 1, 2008.

Bibliography

Holder, Larry. "Bush Says He's Unfazed by Reports from College Days." *Biloxi Sun-Herald,* October 12, 2007.

———. "Bush Vows to Focus on Football: He Wants to Simplify Life." McClatchy-Tribune Business News, March 19, 2008.

Jenkins, Lee. "Reggie Bush's Bootleg Series." *New York Times,* November 30, 2005.

King, Peter. "Reggie Redefined." *Sports Illustrated,* October 20, 2008.

Klein, Gary. "USC Says It Can't Respond; Top Officials on Video Say They Won't Get in Way of Ongoing Mayo and Bush Inquiry." *Los Angeles Times,* June 12, 2009.

Lapointe, Joe. "Bush May Finally Become a Star." *New York Times,* February 6, 2010.

Libby, Brian. "Back 2 Schoolin'." *Men's Fitness,* September 2005.

Mandel, Stewart. "No More Beating Around Bush." *Sports Illustrated,* May 30, 2007. Available online. URL: http://sportsillustrated.cnn.com/2007/writers/stewart_mandel/05/29/cfb.mailbag.

Markazi, Arash. "More Than Just Numbers." *Sports Illustrated,* November 25, 2005.

Martel, Brett. "'I'm Not a Bust': After Two Seasons of Modest Success, Saints' Reggie Bush Sets High Goals for 2008." *St. Louis Post-Dispatch,* August 24, 2008.

McClure, Vaughn. "Bush Move Is Past; Bears' Urlacher Praises Saints' 'Dynamic' Talent." *Chicago Tribune,* December 11, 2008.

McDermott, Mike. "NFL Camp News Roundup: More Injuries to Report." *Providence Journal,* August 5, 2009.

McKay, Hollie. "Kim Kardashian's First Date with Reggie Bush . . . In a Car Wash." FoxNews.com, February 8, 2010.

Bibliography

Milhoces, Gary. "For Saints, Rushing and Defense Must Catch Up to the Air Game." *USA Today*, August 9, 2009.

Miller, Jonathan. "Reggie Bush Interview: The Heisman Trophy Winner Talks New Orleans and Going No. 2." IGN Sports, May 1, 2006. Available online. URL: http://sports.ign.com/articles/704/704035p1.html.

Murphy, Austin. "Bush Came to Shove." *Sports Illustrated*, December 12, 2005.

Pasquarelli, Len. "Sources: Torn Knee Ligament Could Force Bush Out for Season." ESPN.com, December 8, 2007. Available online. URL: http://sports.espn.go.com/nfl/news/story?id=3145712.

Pompei, Dan. "McAllister-Bush a Deadly Combination: Saints Using Two-Headed Running Back Duo Effectively." NBC Sports.com, December 12, 2006. Available online. URL: http://nbcsports.msnbc.com/id/16176533.

Robinson, Jon. "Reggie Talks Ratings: Was Reggie Bush Underrated in Madden '07? He Certainly Thinks So." IGN Sports, May 9, 2007. Available online. URL: http://sports.ign.com/articles/786/786766p1.html.

Schrotenboer, Brent. "Greatness Suits Him." *San Diego Union-Tribune*, December 8, 2005.

———. "Bush's Conquest Is No Contest." *San Diego Union-Tribune*, December 11, 2005.

Silver, Michael. "The Party's In New Orleans." *Sports Illustrated*, October 23, 2006.

Traina, Jimmy. "Q&A: Kim Kardashian Interview." *SI.com*, March 28, 2008. Available online. URL: http://sportsillustrated.cnn.com/2008/extramustard/03/27/kardashian.qa.

Walker, Ben. "Who Dat Nation: Super Saints Become America's Team." Associated Press, February 7, 2010. Available online. URL: http://news.yahoo.com/s/ap/20100207/ap_on_sp_fo_ne/fbn_super_bowl_america_s_team.

Weisman, Larry. "Versatile Bush Wants to Make Plays Happen; Entering 3rd Year, Saints Back Seeks a Breakout Season." *USA Today*, September 2, 2008.

Wharton, David. "Hard to Get: Elusive on Field, Less Than Effusive Off It, Bush Just Wants to Play and Seems Nonplussed by All the Fuss." *Los Angeles Times*, December 3, 2004.

———. "Analysis: Bush's Camp Signals Willingness to Fight." *Los Angeles Times*, November 14, 2007.

FURTHER READING

BOOKS

Bisheff, Steve, and Loel Schrader. *Fight On: The Colorful Story of USC Football.* Nashville, Tenn.: Cumberland House Publishing, 2006.

Donnes, Alan. *Patron Saints: How the Saints Gave New Orleans a Reason to Believe.* New York: Center Street/Hachette, 2007.

Marching In: The World Championship New Orleans Saints. Chicago: Triumph Books, 2010.

Yaeger, Don. *Tarnished Heisman: Did Reggie Bush Turn His Final College Season into a Six-Figure Job?* New York: Pocket Books, 2008.

WEB SITES

JockBio.com: Reggie Bush
http://www.jockbio.com/Bios/Bush/Bush_bio.html

NFL: Reggie Bush
http://www.nfl.com/players/reggiebush/profile?id=BUS294963

Official Site of the New Orleans Saints
http://www.neworleanssaints.com

The Official Site of Reggie Bush
http://www.reggiebush.com

DVDS

Before They Were Pros. ESPN, 2008. Includes footage of Bush before he turned pro.

PICTURE CREDITS

PAGE

9:	AP Images	57:	AP Images
12:	AP Images	61:	AP Images
17:	AP Images	69:	© Sports Illustrated/ Getty Images
23:	© Sean Ryan/Maxppp/ Landov	74:	AP Images
26:	AP Images	77:	AP Images
36:	AP Images	84:	AP Images
40:	AP Images	92:	AP Images
43:	AP Images	95:	© Getty Images
47:	AP Images	104:	AP Images

INDEX

A

Acee, Kevin, 8, 22
All-American honors, 35, 46
Allen, Marcus, 22, 33, 35, 50
All-Pro, 22
All-State players, 27
Arizona Cardinals, 83, 96
Associated Press NFL Offensive Rookie of the Year, 70
Associated Press Player of the Year, 46
Atlanta Falcons, 65
Auburn University, 35

B

Barber, Tiki, 76
Barbour, Allen, 20
Baskett, Hank, 101
Baton Rouge Advocate, 83
Beckham, David, 72
Bellotti, Mike, 38
Bennett, Pat, 33
Benson, Tom, 103
Best Damn Sports Show, The, 46
Boldin, Anquan, 83
Bolt, Usain, 82
Brees, Drew
    teammate, 55–56, 58, 66, 68, 79–82, 97, 101, 103
Brinkley, Douglas, 60
Brown, Sheldon, 67–68
Buchanon, Phillip, 81
Burnley, Charles, 48
Bush, Dezhane (sister), 16
Bush, Doniele (sister), 16
Bush Push, 42–44
Bush, Reggie Sr. (father)
    and football, 14–15
    relationship with, 16

C

Canadian Press, 105
Caputo, Marc, 102
Carolina Panthers
    games against, 67, 75, 83, 96
Carroll, Pete
    college coach, 32–34, 38, 42, 44–45, 49, 105
Casillas, Jonathan, 101
charity donations, 94
    in New Orleans, 62–63
Chase, Damon, 28, 46
Chicago Bears, 96
    games against, 68, 70, 83
Chicago Tribune, 52, 70
childhood
    family, 14–19
    and football, 13, 18–23
Ciara, 72
Cleveland Browns, 65
Colston, Marques, 66
Cornwell, David, 89
Curtis, Jake, 38, 54

D

Dabney, Shaneika, 105
Dallas Cowboys, 56, 67, 96
Davis, Anthony, 10, 34
Davis, Terrell, 22
Davis, Vernon, 56
Deitsch, Richard, 52
Denver Broncos, 22, 81
Doak Walker Award, 46
Dorfman, Bob, 90
Dorsett, Tony, 8
Dunn, Warrick, 76

E

education, 18
    college, 7–8, 10, 12, 32–46, 62, 68, 94, 99
    high school, 8, 10, 19, 21, 23–25, 27–32, 54, 62, 68, 75, 99
Electronic Art's NCAA *Football '07* game, 71

Index

endorsements
 commercials, 72
 contracts, 62, 71, 78, 88, 93
ESPN, 36, 65, 76, 81
ESPN Pac-10 Newcomer of the Year, 34

F

Farmer, Sam, 82, 85
Faulk, Marshall, 8, 11, 22, 76
Favre, Brett, 96–97
Ferguson, D'Brickashaw, 56
Fitzpatrick, D.J., 39
Floyd, Tim, 90
Fox News, 91

G

Gameloft, 71
Garrett, Mike, 90
Green Bay Packers, 96
Green Day, 65
Greene, Maurice, 82
Greenstein, Teddy, 52
Gregory, Bob, 49
Gregory, Sean, 45
Griffen, Everson, 44
Griffin, Denise Lewis (mother), 15
 influence of, 16–20
 support of, 13, 21–22, 31–32
Griffin, Jovan (brother), 15–16, 18
Griffin, LaMar (stepfather), 15, 38, 93
 influence of, 16–18, 20
 support of, 13, 21, 28, 31–32, 46
Griffith-Joyner, Florence, 82
Guardian newspaper, 63–64
Guilbeau, Glenn, 103

H

Hack, Damon, 79
Harmonson, Todd, 11
Hartley, Garrett, 97, 101
Haslett, Jim, 57, 63
Heisman Trophy, 35
 return of, 91
 winners, 32–33, 36, 49–51, 73
 winning, 7, 45–46, 50
Helix High School
 football at, 24–25, 27–31, 46
 freshman year, 24–25
 junior year, 25, 27, 29
 senior year, 29–31
 sophomore year, 25
 state championships, 27
 track team, 25
Hilton, Paris, 72
Horn, Joe, 60, 66
Houston Texans, 53–54, 58
Huffington Post, 105
Hurricane Katrina, 11, 55, 59, 63, 100

I

IGN Sports, 53–55, 58
Indianapolis Colts
 games against, 75
 and the Super Bowl, 75, 97–99, 101–102
injuries, 67–68, 104
 knees, 76, 78, 83, 85–88, 98

J

Jacksonville Jaguars, 76
Jarrett, Dwayne, 41
Jenkins, Lee, 22, 24, 28, 33
Johnson, Michael, 82

K

Kansas City Chiefs, 22, 33
Kardashian, Kim
 relationship with, 72–73, 78, 91, 93–94
Kardashian, Robert, 73
Keeping Up with the Kardashians, 72

Index

Kiffin, Lane, 44
King, Peter, 85
Krikorian, Doug, 15

L
Lake, Lloyd, 88–89, 91
Lane, Paul, 21
Lapointe, Joe, 98, 100
Layden, Tim, 68
Leinart, Matt
  teammate, 31, 36–37, 39, 41–42, 45–46, 49–50, 72
Lombardi Trophy, 103
Loomis, Mickey, 80
Los Angeles, 71, 75, 78, 91
Los Angeles Raiders, 22, 82
Los Angeles Times
  articles in, 16, 18, 20–21, 33, 82, 90

M
Make-A-Wish Foundation, 62
Manning, Peyton, 102
Mardi Gras, 102–103
Markazi, Arash
  articles, 10, 12–13, 45, 52, 58, 64
Martel, Brett, 73, 79, 105
Mayo, O.J., 90
Mays, Corey, 41
McAfee, Fred, 63
McAllister, Deuce
  teammate, 55–56, 58, 65–66, 75, 78, 94
McKay, John, 32
media
  attention, 47, 51–52, 73, 76, 89, 91, 98, 100
  criticism, 12, 42, 69, 78, 90, 105
  praise, 10–11, 50
Men's Fitness, 17, 21, 65, 69
Meyer, Matt, 44
Miami Dolphins, 22, 33

Miami Herald, 102
Michaels, Michael, 88–89
Mihoces, Gary, 88
Miller, Jonathan, 54–55
Minneapolis-Star-Tribune, 73
Minnesota Vikings, 73
  games against, 81–82, 96–97
Monday Night Football, 65
Moore, David Leon, 10–11
Moore, Lance, 101
Morstead, Thomas, 101
Murphy, Austin
  articles, 25, 29, 32–34, 42, 44, 48

N
Nagin, Ray, 102
National Football Conference (NFC), 54–55, 95
  championship game, 67–68, 96, 103
National Football League (NFL)
  drafts, 7, 25, 30, 51–56, 58–59, 88
  expansions, 55
  fans, 8, 10, 13, 47, 51, 55–56, 90, 105
  history, 8, 93
  records, 83
  regulations, 62–63
  scouts, 51–52
  style, 64–65, 68
NBA All-Star weekend, 72
NBCSports.com, 66
NCAA, 88–90
Neuheisel, Rick, 30
New Era agency, 88–89
New Orleans, 8, 10–11
  French Quarter, 102
  hurricane, 11, 55, 59, 63, 100
  living in, 62, 71, 75, 78–79, 91, 104
  people of, 59–60, 98, 100, 102–103

Index

New Orleans Saints
  coaches, 56–58, 60–63, 65–66, 76, 80, 88, 100–101, 103
  contracts with, 56, 93, 105
  fans, 55–56, 58–59, 68, 71, 76, 78, 85, 97–98, 100, 102–103, 105
  history, 12, 55–58, 67, 95, 98, 102
  playing for, 7, 10–12, 54–105
  play-offs, 56–57, 61, 66–67, 78, 83, 96, 104
  rookie year, 10–11, 56, 58, 60, 64–70, 78, 86, 94, 104
  and the Super Bowl, 12, 97–103
  Superdome, 63–65, 68, 96–97, 100
  teammates, 55–56, 58, 60, 65–66, 68, 75, 78–82, 93–94, 97, 100–101, 103
  training camps, 79, 87
  Web site, 90, 98, 100
News-Star, 103
New York Giants, 56, 63
  games against, 67
New York Jets, 54, 56
New York Times, 22, 24, 28, 31, 98, 100
NFC. *See* National Football Conference
NFL. See National Football League
North Carolina State, 53
Notre Dame University
  games against, 30–31, 39, 41–44

O

Oakland Raiders, 33, 83
Obama, Barack, 98
Oklahoma State University, 35
Orange Bowl, 35–36
Orange County Register, 11
Oregon University, 38, 48
Ornstein, Mike, 88–90

P

Pac-10 schools, 30
Parade magazine, 29
Payton, Sean
  coach, 56, 58, 60–62, 65–66, 76, 88, 100–101, 103
People magazine, 91
Peterson, Adrian, 73, 82
Philadelphia Eagles, 67–68
Phillips, Jermaine, 81
Pigskin Club of Washington D.C.'S Offensive Player of the Year, 46
Pittsburgh Steelers, 65
Pola, Kennedy, 28, 31
Pompei, Dan, 66
Pop Warner football, 18–1
Porter, Tracy, 97, 102
Pro Bowl, 96

Q

quarterbacks
  famous, 30–31, 39, 41–42, 45, 49, 58, 66, 96–97, 101
Quinn, Brady, 41

R

Reggie Bush Pro Football 2007 game, 71
Reis, Chris, 101
Rice, Jerry, 22, 54
Rice, Condoleezza, 72
Robinson, John, 32
Rose Bowl, 50–52
running back/tailbacks, 32, 44, 62, 86
  best, 7–8, 10, 22, 43, 45–47, 53, 58, 73–74, 76, 83
  carries, 34
  rushing, 20, 27, 29, 34, 51, 65, 67, 75, 78, 94, 96, 103–104

Index

speed, 8, 10–11, 14, 20, 27, 33, 51, 81–82
touchdowns, 20, 25, 27, 29, 39, 42, 50–51, 65–68, 78, 80–82, 85, 94, 96–97, 103–104

S

Salaam, Rashaan, 33
Sanders, Barry, 8, 11, 76
San Diego, California
   growing up in, 13–15, 22, 29, 32, 45, 50, 93
San Diego Chargers, 22
San Diego State University, 22
San Diego Union-Tribune
   articles in, 8, 19–21, 46, 50
San Francisco Chronicle, 38, 54
San Francisco 49ers, 22, 30, 54, 56
   games against, 66
Sartz, Dallas, 33
Sayers, Gale, 8, 11, 51, 78
Schrotenboer, Brent
   articles, 19–20, 23, 27, 30, 46, 93
Scoggins, Chip, 73
Seattle Seahawks, 104–105
Shockey, Jeremy, 101
Simpson, O.J., 73
Sirius Satellite, 71
Smith, Alex, 25, 30, 54
Smith, Doug, 24
Sporting News, 36
Sports Center, 48
Sports Illustrated
   articles, 10, 13, 18, 25, 29, 32–34, 42, 44–46, 48, 51–52, 60–61, 68, 79–80, 85
Sports Marketers' Scouting Report, 90
Stanford University, 30
Stinchcomb, Jon, 79
St. Louis Post-Dispatch, 73
St. Louis Rams, 22, 56

Stoops, Mike, 49
Super Bowl, 22, 70
   champions, 12, 56, 75
   playing in, 97–102
   winning, 102–103
   XLIV, 99–102

T

Tampa Bay Buccaneers
   games against, 75, 80–81, 83, 96
Tarnished Heisman (Yaeger), 89
Taylor, Phil, 10, 94
Tennessee Titans, 64, 75
Texas University, 30, 45, 50–51
Thomas, Pierre, 94, 97, 101, 103
Time magazine, 45, 51
Times-Picayune, 103
Tomlinson, LaDainian, 22–23
Torres, Eva, 35
Touchdown Club of Columbus
   player of the year, 36, 46
Trotter, Jim, 80

U

U2, 65
UCLA, 35
University of Southern California
   controversy at, 12, 42–43, 88–91
   fans, 32, 39, 47
   football at, 7, 28, 31–52, 73, 86, 93, 105
   freshman year, 34
   history, 34, 39
   junior year, 38–39, 41–45, 50
   national championships, 7, 35, 49–51
   sophomore year, 35–37
   teammates, 10, 32–34, 36–37, 39, 41–45, 49–50, 72, 75
University of Utah, 25, 35
University of Virginia, 56

University of Washington, 30
Urlacher, Brian, 68, 70
USA Today
   articles in, 10, 29, 72, 81, 88

V
Van Hook, Donnie, 25, 27, 29

W
Walker, Darius, 41
Walter Camp Player of the Year
   award, 36, 46
Walton, Bill, 30
Washington Redskins, 67
Washington State, 33
Waters, Ricky, 54
Watkins, Todd, 30
Wayne, Reggie, 102
Weis, Charlie, 43
Weisman, Larry, 81

Wharton, David
   articles, 16, 18, 20, 28,
   32–33
White, Charles, 51
White, LenDale
   teammate, 32, 34–35, 44–45,
   50, 75
White, Leon, 30
wide receiver, 8, 22, 66, 83, 101
Williams, Mario, 53
Williams, Ricky, 22, 33
Willingham, Tyrone, 31
Wilson, Gibril, 82

Y
Yaeger, Don
   Tarnished Heisman, 89
Yahoo! Sports, 89
Young, Steve, 22, 54
Young, Vince, 45, 50

ABOUT THE AUTHOR

ADAM WOOG has written many books for adults, young adults, and children. He has a special interest in American history. Woog lives with his wife in Seattle, Washington, and their daughter attends university in Arizona.

VESTAVIA HILLS
LIBRARY IN THE FOREST
1221 MONTGOMERY HWY.
VESTAVIA HILLS, AL 35216
205-978-0155